# *Recovering* THE SOUL

# Walter Fletcher

 PUBLISHED BY STEEPLE BOOKS
www.steeple.com

Steeple**Books** is an evangelical Christian publisher dedicated to bringing God and people together. We believe God's vision for Steeple**Books** is to enable Christian authors to publish biblical, meaningful, and inspirational materials. Steeple**Books** provides editorial, production, marketing, sales, and distribution services for publishers. *For a free catolog of resources from* Steeple**Books**, *please contact us at* www.steeple.com or send an e-mail to info@steeple.com.

*Recovering the Soul - A Call to Spiritual Health*
Copyright © 2005, 2008 by Walter Fletcher

Originally published in the United States by Desert Rivers International, Dallas, Texas, in 2005.

All rights reserved. No portion of this book may be reproduced, stored in a retrieval system, or transmitted in any form or by any means—electronic, mechanical, photocopy, recording, or any other—except for brief quotations in printed reviews, without the prior permission of the publisher.

Except where otherwise indicated, Scripture quotations are taken from New King James Version of the Bible (NKJV) and are used by permission.

Cover design by Tim Triplett

For more information about the author and his ministry, address all correspondence to: Desert Rivers International, 305 Spring Creek Village, Suite 507, Dallas, Texas 75248.

Fletcher, Walter
   Recovering the Soul - A Call to Spiritual Health / by Walter Fletcher.
       p.    cm.
   ISBN 978-0-9821240-1-7 (previously ISBN 0-9709970-0-0)
   Summary: "Using biblical examples from a lifetime of ministry, Walter Fletcher gives a message of hope for those who want to recover their soul's true identity"--Provided by publisher.

   1. Christian life. 2. Self-esteem--Religious aspects--Christianity. 3. Joy--Religious aspects--Christianity. 4. Laughter--Religious aspects--Christianity. 5. Hope--Religious aspects--Christianity. I. Title

   Printed in the United States of America.

# Dedication

To Deede,
My faithful companion and friend,
My co-laborer and greatest fan.

# Recovering THE SOUL
### A Call to Spiritual Health

## Acknowledgments

No one writes a book alone. This book has had a team of collaborators whose personal touch or interest has brought it into being. I wish to acknowledge the following:

To Ken Gire, whose Writer's Workshop and personal follow-up caused me to take the cost and nature of writing seriously.

To Valerie Lumbley, who worked alongside me for years as my faithful assistant rightly discerning the poet and writer *locked inside* "trying to get out", forcing me to take concrete action.

To Norma Anderson and Linda Fletcher, who believed in me as a writer and offered their editorial skills to the project. Their diligence, time and energy have helped to make this book a reality.

To DeVern Fromke, whose quiet wisdom, humility, spiritual "fathering" and friendship for almost two decades have shaped my life for eternity.

To Iris Pearce, a spiritual director in my life, whose counsel and instruction helped to release and embolden me to follow my dreams.

To the friends whose keen interest and generosity have made this project a practical reality.

To my natural family and my spiritual community, whose love and prayers have blanketed this project.

Thank you!

# Recovering THE SOUL
*A Call to Spiritual Health*

## Contents

PROLOGUE          1

The INWARD Journey

| | | |
|---|---|---|
| Chapter One | The Barren Soul | 4 |
| Chapter Two | The Fractured Soul | 11 |
| Chapter Three | The Wounded Soul | 19 |
| Chapter Four | The Scattered Soul | 25 |
| Chapter Five | The Restored Soul | 32 |
| Chapter Six | The Prayerful Soul | 42 |
| Chapter Seven | The Awakened Soul | 50 |
| Chapter Eight | The Worshipful Soul | 59 |

The OUTWARD Call

| | | |
|---|---|---|
| Chapter Nine | The Soul of Revival | 69 |
| Chapter Ten | The Soul of the Church | 77 |
| Chapter Eleven | The Soul of the Kingdom | 84 |

# Recovering THE SOUL
*A Call to Spiritual Health*

## Prologue

This book has been nearly thirty years in the making. Not that I have been writing it for that long. Rather, it has been writing me. I now realize an enormous amount of life experience brings forth wisdom and understanding. Fruit-bearing trees do not grow overnight. Neither does the root life necessary to bring forth the life giving truths of the Spirit of God. Wisdom and understanding must be lived in proportion to the desire that they release the life of God's grace and truth to others.

Today, many in the Body of Christ have fallen upon hard times spiritually. They are ensnared in a spurious trap, believing that giving assent to truth is the same as possessing the truth. They believe they can achieve spiritual maturity in "Ten Easy Steps," or installment plans. They want spiritual growth without the process, pain or struggle. And yet, all of life (even nature) teaches us the opposite. It is in this process of development that we discover our true soul; that soul identity that enables us to pursue our purpose in life. It is the soul, that part of our being, which gives us our own personality, likes and dislikes, our will and volition. It is our soul that has been creatively formed in order that it can be both informed and transformed by God. Thus in cooperation with the Spirit of God and the Word of God, the soul reaches out for his or her destiny.

All too often, if we are not alert to its danger, we can find ourselves mimicking our culture, which does not take God seriously. A culture that devalues the place of God in life will slowly erode a desire for godliness in order to deform, defeat and ultimately destroy the true soul of an individual. However, the sincere follower after God will strive to recover his or her soul, albeit it may mean an uphill battle or require that they swim upstream against the currents of our time. There is what Richard Foster has called the "muchness and many" and the mad clutching and grabbing that goes along with the false illusions of life. These illusions often take on the appearance of power, wealth, fame, and success.

Jesus offered His followers an alternative to these dangerous illusions, when He said,

> *Whoever desires to come after me, let him deny himself, and take up his cross, and follow Me. For whoever desires to save his life will lose it, but whoever loses his life for My sake and the gospel's will save it. For what will it profit a man if he gains the whole world, and loses his own soul? Or what will a man give in exchange for his soul?* (Mark 8:34-37).

This book is for those who want to "recover" their souls; those who are honest with themselves and are hungry seekers after God. This book is about Christian Spirituality; a way in which we can stay attached to God and attentive to

God at work in our life and in the world around us, and in which God has been pleased to place us. It is my sincere desire that it will help in the process of discovering how we can keep in step with the rhythm and timing of His purpose for our life, rather than the "ticking and timing" of the world around us.

I have no false illusions that I have written anything in this book that has not been said hundreds of times by others much more experienced along the spiritual path towards greater heart knowledge of God. Therefore, it is my sincere hope that what is written here will open perhaps a window into the issue of soul care and growth, allowing a fresh breeze to blow into the room of the heart, and a cup of cold water to quench the thirsty soul in the name of the Lord.

No one has a corner on the market of truth and knowledge in the things of God. I am content as a fellow pilgrim to leave a little room for mystery on our soul's journey towards Him.

Walter Fletcher<br>
Dallas, Texas<br>
September 2008

# The Barren SOUL

## Chapter One

*O God, you are my God; early will I seek You;*
*My soul thirsts for you in a dry and thirsty land*
*Where there is no water* (Psalm 63:1).

She was not the one we were told to expect. I, along with a small group of people from Dallas, Texas, had traveled halfway around the world to do a Prayer Walking Tour through the Holy Land. We were expecting a male tour guide, but we learned that at the last moment, due to an emergency, he was called away. One thing I've learned is, with God there are no unforeseen circumstances or emergencies. The gentleman was replaced by Deborah (not her real name).

There Deborah stood waiting for us weary and sleepy pilgrims. We had traveled hours and through several time zones getting to our destination, and then by our tour bus. She was a striking figure, almost six feet tall and very slender. She was well tanned from the middle-eastern sun; her shoulder length hair was parted in the middle. She wore a full-length, olive-toned dress, which was covered with a khaki safari-type jacket, and brown and green canvas hiking boots. But the most striking thing to me was that, behind a dark pair of sunglasses was the most beautiful, warm smile assuring us of our welcome to the Holy Land. And I heard the Lord whisper to my heart, "I have given you a faithful guide in the Land."

This was soon to be proven true, far beyond anything our little group could have hoped. Because of Deborah's rich knowledge of the biblical history of the land, as well as her easy demeanor and willingness to be flexible as our prayer team sought the Lord's "daily plan" and directions, we saw and accomplished more than we could have ever imagined. Although that is a story for another time.

One of the highlights still fresh in my memory is the first day's tour to the nature reserve where many of the plants, trees, and shrubs from biblical days have been preserved for tourists. I was amazed to see the variety and beauty of the greenery, plants, shrubs, flowers, and trees that are native to the present mysterious, arid, desert-like surroundings. Our guide explained the fertile secret: "In order for the people to live in such desert conditions and be able to maintain the plants, trees and vibrant agricultural crops that you see, the farmers have learned a special irrigation method. They use tiny little irrigation pipes that drip only the amount necessary to sustain the crops, thus practicing a conservation method of the precious water supply. These methods have been so perfected that by rotating the various types of crops, they can get as many as four different harvests in one year."

While this fresh insight and revelation was still sinking into our newly enlightened minds, Deborah went on to say something else that was even more valuable to our team: "The desert can be deceptive in its beauty. Even when a breeze is blowing, making the air feel cooler, you can still dehydrate very quickly. So think of the irrigation method and be sure to carry your water bottle along with you wherever you go, taking frequent sips of water to stay hydrated."

Like the desert, our soul can become dry, parched and barren as we travel along our pilgrim journey in God. It can happen imperceptibly, especially if you are a regular churchgoer! You can be ever so punctual in your religious observances—Sunday morning, perhaps a mid-week service. You clock in and clock out, as it were, with such a faithful dutifulness. Then one day it happens, you wake up to this dull, spiritual ache deep on the inside, a thirst that cannot be easily defined nor quickly dismissed.

If you have the courage and honesty, you will not ignore the internal promptings. This cry from the center of your being could be a call to let you know that "it is time for you to go deeper in God." You may even have a little conversation with yourself that goes something like this: "What is the matter with me? I know I love God, I say my prayers, I pay my tithes... attend church regularly. And yet I no longer am satisfied with my 'religious' routine. There has got to be more."

Many people have come to me over the years expressing similar distressing sentiments. After listening patiently, I first assure them that they have not "lost their salvation" or somehow "backslidden" from God. The fact that they came to see me is a clue that they are probably in a spiritual growth spurt and experiencing all the symptoms that go along with it. Deep within their being, as it were, God has "pushed a button" that says it is time to get to know God better. Somehow people also know that if they respond to this call, they will come to know themselves better as well. I'm tempted to say to them at this point (though I don't), "Welcome to Friendship with God 101"! But instead, I let them know that the problems that have brought them to this crisis (natural or spiritual) are probably an indication that God has invited them on a journey of friendship with Him. He longs to know them in a deeper, more intimate way just as much as they have a thirst to know Him. It is, as it were, a "deep calling unto deep." They are responding to the echo of God's call on the inside.

Throughout the scriptures we find God initiating friendships. The Word declares, "Enoch walked with God," "Noah walked with God," "Abraham walked with God," and others like Moses and David all were called to be friends of God. They teach us the way of friendship into the heart of God. This is a vital lesson.

In times of barrenness, you must maintain a right focus. David cried out in the midst of his own heart thirst, "O God, You are my God." He refused to be ruled by his emotions, which could cause him to tend to wander off, seeking something else (or someone else!). Rather he stayed before the face of God, in His presence, with his spiritual dissatisfaction.

Getting our relationship with God out of focus is a sure way to lose sight of the path that leads us to our soul's true quest—a greater knowledge of God. Like David, as an act of focused faith, we must declare, "God, You are my God!" Perhaps, for David (and us) no feelings arose in this declaration. Nothing seems to have changed outwardly, nor was there any apparent movement inwardly. But he centered himself, his affections and desires on God alone.

I heard Bruce Olson, the great missionary author of Bruchko, tell of his experience in encountering the Motilone Indians of the Rain Forests of Colombia. He was trying to write down their language, which never had been done before, and was struggling to find a word for "faith". One day while watching the people tie their sleeping hammocks high up in the trees and rest in them without the fear of falling, he had his definition of faith! He wrote, "Faith means to tie one's hammock into God, resting one's whole weight and trust upon Him Who is unseen."

I have found when I do not have any great sense of "God moments" in my life, I too must "tie my hammock into God," knowing that He will hold me. I must anchor myself to God until He shows Himself to me in this new adventure of trust. The psalmist declared, "When my heart is overwhelmed lead me to the Rock that is higher than I." When you cannot see where you are going, and you do not know what tomorrow brings, "tie yourself into God". Begin to trust Him with your future in a new way.

This new relationship of trust in God can be developed by trying this spiritual exercise. Come to God, knowing that He sees your heart longing and desire for more of Him. Set a time and a place to meet with Him. Do not come to impress Him, nor others, with how spiritual you are; but as Jesus said, "Go into your closet and shut the door." In other words, leave the world with its prying eyes outside. Come as you are. Come for yourself alone. And above all, come with a hunger and thirst to meet with God alone.

He has promised to exalt us at the appointed time from a posture of humility. In the place of honesty, God makes Himself known. He said, "Be still and know that I am God." God dwells in the stillness of our heart. The prophet Isaiah wrote, "In quietness and confidence shall be your strength." Try to let go of the noise inside of you—fear, frustration, worry, deadlines. Then in that place of stillness, let the quietness and peace of God that is around you in those moments begin to seep into your soul. It may not happen immediately. However, if you will continue to meet with God in this way, you will soon experience the quietness of God around you that has become the quietness of God within you.

Another helpful practice is to do as the prophet exhorted, "Take with you words" (Hosea 14:2). What "words" might you bring? The best words are the scriptures. Words and phrases from the Bible help us to know what we need to pray. We use these words, making them our words, offering them to God as the cry, desire, and intent of our hearts. These words can mirror our soul's condition and cause the refreshing promises of His word to water our parched souls.

In this honest interaction with God, we discover our personal need rather than try to place a finger on the problem outside of us. The "desert" fathers and mothers believed it was more important that we learn how to fight the enemies within, rather than the ones without. That purgation in the desert is the true essence of the beginning of our recovering of the soul. We find Paul's words in agreement, "Let us cleanse ourselves from all filthiness of the flesh and spirit, perfecting holiness in the fear of God" (2 Corinthians 7:1).

It is by and through the agency of the Word of God that we are washed through and through. Our Lord Jesus tells us that if we would see and know God more intimately, purity is a necessary step. "Blessed are the pure in heart for they shall see God" (Matthew 5:8).

The soul's journey, albeit through the barren desert, is right into the heart of God. Only in God can we find our true self. Only in Jesus Christ can we find true refreshing. He said, "If anyone is thirsty let him come to Me and drink. He who believes in Me, as the scripture said, 'From his innermost being will flow rivers of living water'" (John 7:37-38 NASB).

Weary and barren soul, let your bucket down into the river of life in Jesus Christ. He alone can satisfy your real thirst.

# The Fractured SOUL

## Chapter Two

*By faith Jacob, when he was dying, blessed each of the sons of Joseph, and worshiped, leaning upon the top of his staff* (Hebrews 11:21).

My wife, Deede, and I have had the joy of traveling in many parts of the world. One of our favorite spots is England. We love the genuine friendliness of the people and the beautiful rolling hills that can be seen as we travel through the countryside. We also enjoy the sights of the homes and ancient castles that dot the countryside, many of them hundreds of years in age. Accompanying the homes are farms and pasture lands for grazing sheep and cattle.

Once when we, along with some newly found friends, were traveling from London heading toward beautiful Northumberland, we spotted a flock of sheep close by the roadside. We stopped to get a closer look at them. Initially when we made our approach, they did not stir much. But when Deede began to talk to them, they suddenly backed away and bolted in every direction. The problem was they were not familiar with her voice. In just a moment the owner of the sheep came out and called them, and quickly they moved together and rallied close to their shepherd.

Recognizing the shepherd's voice is especially important for the protection of each sheep. Without His presence, the sheep are quite vulnerable and defenseless. I have been told that if a newborn lamb does not learn to stay close to the rest of the flock and the shepherd, the shepherd may have to break its leg, which is then set and bandaged. While recovering, it is placed upon the shoulders of the shepherd and carried there until the leg has mended. Afterward, that lamb will follow very close to the shepherd, often closer than the rest of the flock.

Many of God's people have had a similar experience spiritually. No, their legs may not have been broken in a physical way, but they have known what it is to have to be healed from a "fracture" of the soul—a fracture caused by a tendency to stray from the path of the Shepherd, Jesus Christ. Simon Peter wrote, "For you were like sheep going astray, but have now returned to the Shepherd and Overseer of your souls."

Perhaps this is the meaning of David's words, himself a shepherd, when he wrote, "Make me to hear joy and gladness, that the bones which Thou hast broken may rejoice" (Psalm 51:8 KJV). This was a psalm of repentance after his adulterous affair and his "kingly" order to have the woman's husband killed in battle. But on the heels of these wicked deeds, God forgives David. Now, like a lamb that had strayed from his Shepherd, he uses the imagery of a broken leg that has been mended, to describe his spiritual condition. He wants to experience the joy of God's salvation once more. Again, Simon Peter may have recalled his own experience of being brought back into fellowship and to his apostleship after his denial of his Lord (See John 21).

Of all the people in the scriptures who experienced the loving, healing touch of his Shepherd, Jacob stands out the most. His record is the tale of one man's journey from a fractured soul to being made whole by God.

Jacob enters the stage of biblical history as the product of an answered prayer that his father Isaac received. Isaac had married Rebekah, apparently later in life than some. She was barren and unable to have children, but Isaac believed that God could do a miracle and open her womb so she could bear a child. He prayed and God rewarded his faith, not with one child but with twin boys.

Rebekah soon discovered that these boys were different than typical twins. Esau, the firstborn, was said to be "red and hairy all over." He was a true out-doors-man, hunter and man of the field. His brother, Jacob, on the other hand was not at all hairy. Apparently, he was a bit of a mama's boy and hung around the tent. He also learned to cook.

Isaac, the father, loved Esau; however, Rebekah loved Jacob. Which inevitably set the stage for what today we call a "dysfunctional family". No love was lost between them, as they were natural competitors. One day Esau returned from a hunting trip with no game to show for his efforts. Exhausted and famished, he smelled the pot of red stew Jacob had fixed, and asked if he might have some. Jacob, whose business skills were developing, agreed to give him some of his stew if Esau would sell him his birthright. Esau foolishly agreed to do so, and lived to regret it.

Time passed. Isaac was now old and feeble and nearly blind. He called for Esau and asked him to go hunt for his favorite game. When Esau returned and prepared it, he was to bring it to his father and receive the blessing of the firstborn. While eavesdropping, Rebekah learned of the plan. She told Jacob and they entered into an elaborate charade of deception so that he might receive the blessing of Isaac, rather than Esau, who should rightly receive the inheritance. The plan worked without a hitch. His father, unsuspecting, blessed Jacob with the blessing of the firstborn.

When Esau returned and found out what Jacob had done and how he had received the blessing that belonged to him, he went ballistic, promising to kill his brother after his father's death. Jacob knew that his brother would make good on his threat, so he packed his few belongings and ran for his life.

Although Jacob was on the run, he still had the blessing of the firstborn. He valued the blessing because he understood that in the blessing of the firstborn is the right of the double portion of the inheritance, as well as the right to rule in the family.

I do not think Jacob is much different from most of us. Many people come to the blessing of God's salvation in Jesus Christ, enticed by the benefits. The gospel has often been presented as an "insurance policy". We give over our sins and bad habits, and God gives us His peace, joy and other benefits. In the end, heaven is our home. From a certain angle, we can prove that the scriptures offer these things to those who belong to Jesus Christ. But this does not go far enough. Heaven may be ours at the end of faith, but God has a desire and plan for our lives as well. Jacob's life reminds us of this fact.

God's goal is not merely that we receive all the wonderful benefits of Calvary. Rather as Paul puts it, "For the love of Christ compels us, because we judge thus: that if One died for all, then all died; and He died for all, that those who live should live no longer for themselves, but for Him who died for them and rose again" (2 Corinthians 5:14-15).

Jacob, like many today, had received the blessing in his life, but it was still all about him, not about God. Esau, on the other hand, is another story. He was angry enough to kill his brother for what he had done, but he had not come to terms with a deeper issue. Esau gave up the birthright, which was his as the firstborn, for he did not value it spiritually. Therefore, in a time of physical need, his natural lusts for human, momentary satisfaction overrode his spiritual desires. John warns us, "Do not love the world or the things in the world. If anyone loves the world, the love of the Father is not in him. For all that is in the world—the lust of the flesh, the lust of the eyes, and the pride of life—is not of the Father but is of the world. And the world is passing away, and the lust of it; but he who does the will of God abides forever" (1 John 2:15-17).

Although Esau had been, like many today, around the things of God, he did not value them in his life. Somehow, he grew indifferent to the blessings of God and was moving further and further away from the things of God by his choices. Finally, through his bitterness and resentment of his brother Jacob, he openly rebelled against his parents, and ultimately God. The writer of the letter to the Hebrews wrote, "Pursue peace with all people, and holiness, without which no one will see the Lord: looking carefully lest anyone fall short of the grace of God; lest any root of bitterness springing up cause trouble, and by this many become defiled; lest there be any fornicator or profane person like Esau, who for one morsel of food sold his birthright. For you know that afterward, when he wanted to inherit the blessing, he was rejected, for he found no place for repentance, though he sought it diligently with tears" (Hebrews 12:14-17).

But let's go back to Jacob. Jacob's running was leading him on a great adventure and to several self-discoveries. First, he discovered that you cannot outrun God. While running from Esau, he bumped into God. Somewhere between Jacob's home and that of his uncle Laban, the LORD God appeared to him in a dream. He saw a ladder let down from heaven with angels ascending and descending. The LORD God spoke to Jacob assuring him of the fact that the covenant God of his fathers, Abraham and Isaac, was his as well. Awakened from his sleep with the frightful awareness that the awesome presence of God was there, he established his stone pillow as a memorial pillar unto God, calling it Bethel – House of God.

If you have ever had a special moment with God, you know that you encounter Him in a unique way. You find yourself making fresh new decisions to follow God. You move closer to His side. You come to believe that "God is a rewarder of them who diligently seek Him" (Hebrews 11:6).

The second thing Jacob discovered was the law of sowing and reaping. Paul wrote, "Whatever a man sows, that he will also reap" (Galatians 6:7). In coming to live with his uncle Laban, Jacob discovered someone who was as cunning a trickster as he was himself! Laban tricked Jacob into marrying Leah, his oldest daughter, before he could marry Rachel, whom he really loved. His wages were changed ten different times. Finally, after twenty years of this trickery, Jacob took his wives and children, determined to return to his homeland.

The final scene of Jacob's fractured soul, as it were, was the healing by God. Jacob was on his way home. He had put more and more distance between him and his uncle Laban, but he had not put enough distance between himself and Esau. He heard that Esau was coming to find him and no doubt would make good on his threat to kill him.

What did he do? He divided his family and fortune, sending his servants ahead with presents for Esau, hoping to put more and more distance between them. Then he did one more thing… he crossed the river Jabok. Now he was alone. But not entirely, for God was there.

Aloneness is not the same as loneliness. Jacob discovered what everyone sooner or later discovers. It is often in times of separation from people and things like family, fame and fortune that God is waiting to meet with us. God waited for over twenty years for this encounter. An angel wrestled with Jacob until the breaking of the day. Jacob seemingly had won the match; he still had a hold of the angel. But the truth was the other way around… the angel of the Lord had Jacob!

Jacob was determined not to let go of the angel until he was blessed by him. This was one final attempt on Jacob's part to control the outcome. The angel of the LORD said, "Okay, I'll bless you. But you'll have to tell me your name," knowing that in the Hebrew understanding, one's name equaled his nature or character. Jacob had to confess who he was. His name means "trickster", "supplanter", "deceiver". And in that moment of confession, God said, "No more shall you be called Jacob but Israel, meaning 'a prince having power with God.'"

Jacob received a new name and a new nature from God. When the sun dawned upon him, he crossed over the river to meet Esau and his family. Jacob was a changed man. Because the angel of the Lord had touched his thigh, he would walk with a limp the rest of his life. He had to learn to lean upon a staff.

That staff would come to represent more than a crutch. Rather it represented a man who had learned from his fracture, to trust. What he needed was an abiding trust and dependency on God and not on himself. He learned that the true secret of his strength and success was the touch of God in one's life. Even when he was old in years, he found strength enough to lean upon his staff and speak into the destiny of his sons. This was the lesson he learned. This was the legacy he left. We, too, must put no confidence in our flesh; we must come to trust God as our sufficiency lest we, like Jacob, unwittingly choose our fracture over our God-appointed limp. May we learn to lean wholeheartedly in faith upon God, becoming "strong in the Lord and in the power of His might" (Ephesians 6:10).

# The Wounded SOUL

## Chapter Three

*He was despised and rejected by men, a man of sorrows and acquainted with grief. And we hid, as it were, our faces from Him; He was despised, and we did not esteem Him. Surely He has borne our grief and carried our sorrows; yet we esteemed Him stricken, smitten by God and afflicted. But he was wounded for our transgressions, He was bruised for our iniquities; the chastisement for our peace was upon Him, and by His stripes we are healed* (Isaiah 53:3-6).

He collapsed into my arms and sobbed like a little child. He was in his mid-forties. I had never experienced this before, although I have many times since. At first I was a little self-conscious, but I soon got over this, knowing that something very profound was taking place in this dear man's life. Something I had said during the men's retreat had affected him deeply.

Finally he regained his composure, and told me his story. "For the first ten years of my life I thought my name was a curse word. Whenever my father called me, he would use swear words. But while you were speaking… it is the first time in my life I have had the courage to come forward to get this hurt and shame out of my life."

What was his problem? The real problem was that the boy had become a man physically, yet he was still suffering from emotional blows received while he was a child. He had no one, as a child, to make him feel wanted, safe or secure. He had no one to protect him from the verbal blows or to show him how to ward off these repeated psychological violations.

]We prayed together and when we had finished, his whole countenance had changed, radiating peace and joy. He left that day a free man, able to walk out of the prison house of his shame, confusion and wounds.

Although I do not remember the dear man's name, I am reminded of the fact that he represents many thousands of others, men and women, who have been traumatized in life. They have been physically or emotionally abused, or both. They are survivors; they are the "walking wounded". Or as someone described his experience, "like a helium balloon that never quite soars, getting entangled in the branches of trees on their way up". Life, for them, is what happened while they were on their way to doing something else!

Each of us may experience many types of wounds in life. Denying them does not change their reality in our life. Only as we have the courage to take them out of the closet, as it were, and hold them up to the light of God can we name them for what they are and begin the process of healing the wounded soul.

We can be traumatized by those who are closest to us. Family members, whether intended or not, often wound us, and vice-versa. The prophet Zechariah describes one who had been "wounded in the house of my friends" (Zechariah

13:6). Sometimes emotional and physical wounds received from those we should be able to trust and feel safe with are more devastating than wounds given by a stranger.

The story of Jabez, found in the scriptures, has become well known among this generation after the release of Bruce Wilkinson's national best-selling book, *The Prayer of Jabez*. He apparently sustained a wound to his soul from his mother. "His mother called him, Jabez, saying, 'Because I bore him in pain'" (1 Chronicles 4:9).

Culturally, a Jewish parent named his child with hope of good character and potential. Naming him "a pain, or one who causes pain or sorrow" left its stigma upon his psyche. I can only imagine what his childhood and young adulthood must have been like in a community that valued the naming of children for their potential. Who wanted to be his friend? Who wanted to hire him for a job? After all, who wants "a pain or sorrow" on their team? But one day, Jabez awoke to the reality that he was not the sum total of what others thought about him, and he was not willing to walk under the shadow of this dark cloud of rejection, of being a failure with a false identity.

What did he do? He brought this wound upon his soul into the light of God's presence. He refused to accept the evaluation of others about him, determining that the only real evaluation that mattered was God's. We read, "And Jabez called on the God of Israel, saying 'Oh, that You would bless me indeed, and enlarge my territory, that your hand would be with me, and that you would keep me from evil, that I may not cause pain!' So God granted him what he requested" (1 Chronicles 4:10). God heard his petition and granted his request. Jabez no longer walked under guilt or shame! He became known as a man of great honor and respect in his day and a witness for us today.

Until we, like Jabez, are willing to expose our wound before God, knowing that He is our true Father who loves us unconditionally, we will not receive the healing we desire.

Joseph experienced wounds from his own brothers. They were envious and jealous of him because of the dreams he had shared of ruling over them, and because of the favoritism his father gave him. They take him, ignoring his piteous cries, and put him down into a pit. Then they sell him as a slave to Midianites heading for Egypt; from there he is sold again to Potiphar. While working under Potiphar's roof, the master's wife, who cannot seduce Joseph sexually, seeks to punish him by accusing him of attempted rape. This lands him in Pharaoh's prison. Joseph's life seems to be going down, down, down!

At this point, we might begin asking ourselves, "What's a nice guy like 'Joe' doing in a place like this?" The answer is that God was working His plan for Joseph's life. Apart from the momentary discomfort, God was going to vindicate His servant and bring glory and honor to His name. Every wound he received would prove to be redemptive in the end. God is the only One who can take the things that have been so horrible and tragic in our lives and turn them for our good. Joseph's wounds, due to envy, rejection, and slander were not taking him further down in God; they were actually lifting him higher in God, and soon this would be apparent to all. The psalmist records the rest of Joseph's story.

> *He sent a man before them—Joseph—who was sold as a slave. They hurt his feet with fetters, he was laid in irons. Until the time that his*

*word came to pass, the Word of the LORD tested him. The king sent and released him, the ruler of the people let him go free. He made him lord of his house, and ruler of all his possessions, to bind princes at his pleasure, and teach his elders wisdom* (Psalm 105:17-22).

Joseph refused to let his circumstances get the better of him. He did not minimize what his brothers had done to him. It hurt! But rather than getting bitter or getting revenge upon his brothers, he chose to become better. He confronted them with truth, but acknowledged that his wounding experiences had a higher purpose. "You meant evil against me; but God meant it for good, in order to bring it about as it is this day, to save many people alive" (Genesis 50:20). Looking through a larger window, he saw the purposes of God.

Only as we learn how to absorb the blows that were meant to bring us down are we prepared to allow God's grace to transform the blows into blessings. Believe that in spite of your test, God means it for a testimony. The iron that was upon Joseph's feet worked iron into his soul; the godly character was necessary to go with the authority to rule that he would receive in time of famine in Egypt.

Wounds can also come from wrong choices. Sin always leaves its marks upon our life. The woman "caught in adultery" was wounded by the shame and exposure of her deed. According to the Law of Moses, she was worthy of a death sentence. But by the grace and forgiveness of Jesus Christ, she was absolved of her illicit past, allowing her to embrace a future filled with the light of His love (read John 8:1-12).

Peter was deeply wounded by his loss of courage to stand up and acknowledge his allegiance to Jesus in His hour of trial. But the Lord had mercy upon him. Jesus forgave him and fully restored him, not only as a friend, but also as a chief apostle. Through confession, his wounds of fear and guilt were replaced with divine love and a bold faith (John 21).

God sent Jesus Christ, His Son, into the world to bring healing to the wounded soul. To borrow an expression from Henri Nouwen, considered one of the leading spiritual writers of the 20th Century, Jesus became the Wounded Healer for you and me. He bore every wound upon His back at the whipping post, and He is able to heal us of every wound we have suffered.

Perhaps the greatest wounds God heals us from are shame and guilt. Hear this good news: God is a Destroyer of shame! He has promised, "Do not fear, for you will not be ashamed; neither be disgraced, for you will not be put to shame; for you will forget the shame of your youth" (Isaiah 54:4).

You can be healed of your past and embrace your future in God. He says, "For I know the thoughts that I think toward you… thoughts of peace and not of evil, to give you a future and a hope" (Jeremiah 29:11).

Go! Live in the love, peace, forgiveness, and freedom won for you by Jesus Christ. As Paul wrote, "Stand fast therefore in the liberty by which Christ has made us free, and do not be entangled again with a yoke of bondage" (Galatians 5:1).

# The Scattered SOUL

## Chapter Four

*A double-minded man is unstable in all his ways* (James 1:8).

*No one can serve two masters; for either he will hate one and love the other, or else He will be loyal to the one And despise the other. You cannot serve God and mammon* (Matthew 6:24).

I am not an avid movie goer. But I have become a better movie watcher. I suppose the reason is that I stopped going as the proverbial "movie critic," taking every scene and character apart and filtering them through my analytical process to determine the outcome of the movie. Often I was correct in my assessment. However, I came to realize that I had not really understood some of the movie's "story-line" value. Meaning that the writer or director is attempting to show us, the viewer, the "stuff" that makes us who we are. We all face the ups and downs of life and, at times, pursue contradictory behavior. And again, sometimes through the story's narrative process, we are surprised when we realize who proves to be the hero in the story. In this way if we are attuned, we find ourselves in the story.

Often in a good movie, the hero of the story proves to be a kind of "Christ-figure" character. This person is often counted as unimportant to the rest of the family or community, because he acts different or is seemingly a little "odd" in his ways. Therefore, he is dismissed and discounted as a person. Then, suddenly! There is a transition in the story. A crisis hits the family or the town folk. As the plot unfolds, the individual, who was of no account in the eyes of others, proves to hold the key which unlocks the door that "saves the day"! It may be a word or a gesture of kindness that proves to be an epiphany, a dawning of hope or healing, that changes the catastrophic situation into something meant for good in the end. Those moments give us, the viewers, a window into our own human nature. We find ourselves in each story.

For example, in the dramatic and engaging epic movie of *The Last Samurai*, Tom Cruise plays the Civil War hero, Captain Nathan Algren. Captain Algren is troubled and tormented in conscience by his participation in an American Indian massacre where a whole village of unarmed women and children were slaughtered while the men were away on a hunting party.

Algren had tried repeatedly, yet unsuccessfully, to drown the memory of these events in a bottle of whisky, and became an alcoholic. A friend located him in this condition and made him aware of a "job" opportunity. Some high-ranking Japanese officials who wanted them to come to Japan and train their military in new American "strategies of war," were soliciting their military skills. Algren agreed to take on the job, in hopes of escaping his nightmares of the massacre in which he took part. He more or less became "a gun for hire". Little did he know that this trip would prove to be a chance for redemption.

While he helped to train and then lead a regiment of Japanese soldiers against the fierce Samurai warriors, he was wounded and miraculously spared death. Instead he was taken as a prisoner of war and kept alive by Katsumoto, a Samurai warrior and leader. He was taken back to the Samurai village, where his physical and emotional wounds slowly healed. Captain Algren and Katsumoto formed a strange friendship, as both were students of the strategies of war. And Algren developed a deep appreciation for the lifestyle of the Japanese people.

Algren soon was allowed to roam about the village with a soldier escort. He became enchanted by the beauty and the simplicity of the people and its culture. He recorded in his diary, "They are an intriguing people. From the moment they wake, they devote themselves to the perfection of whatever they pursue. I have never seen such discipline." Eventually, he was allowed to join the other Samurai warriors and train with them, learning of their way of fighting and, of course, the use of the Samurai sword.

They practice their swordsmanship with a stick. Day after day as Algren practiced, he received blow upon blow from his opponent. He could not figure out why he was repeatedly defeated. Then one day, Katsumoto's son, who had come to appreciate Algren's willingness to learn, leans over him while he is still on the ground from the opponent's blow and says, "Too many minds." To which Algren in consternation says, "Too many minds?" The young man answers him, "You mind sword, you mind people watching, and you mind the enemy... too many minds."

Suddenly! The light bulb comes on. In order to defeat his opponent, he would have to shed those other "minds" and maintain a single focus. From that moment on, his skills improved. He became recognized and respected as a worthy Samurai warrior.

Often, like Algren, "too many minds" hinders our progress in God. Our souls become scattered as we let our gaze drift to things that do not benefit our journey with God. James wrote, "A double-minded man is unstable in all his ways" (James 1:8). The original is not double minded but "double souled".

Double-souled people never make progress in their Christian walk, because they are forever taking two steps forward and three steps back. They are like John Bunyan's character, "Mr. Facing Both Ways," who in Bunyan's classic work, Pilgrim's Progress, lacks the stamina to go forward because he is always looking over his shoulder to see what is behind.

The children of Israel did not make it into the promised land until forty years had elapsed, although they could have arrived in less than two weeks. Why? Because every time they got into a difficulty or challenge regarding provision, they would moan and complain about how it would have been better if they had stayed in Egypt. They quickly forgot the four hundred years of slavery and harsh treatment under Pharaoh. And they subsequently forgot the miraculous provision of God. They were double souled.

If you are not willing to forget the past and embrace the destiny that God has ahead, you will never make any headway toward your tomorrow. As an old proverb observes, "The turtle makes no progress unless he is willing to stick his neck out." The apostle Peter admonishes that we need diligence and focus in order to grow in the things of God.

> ... giving, all diligence, add to your faith virtue, to virtue knowledge, to knowledge self-control, to self-control perseverance, to perseverance godliness, to godliness brotherly kindness, and to brotherly kindness love. For if these things are yours and abound, you will be neither barren nor unfruitful in the knowledge of our Lord Jesus Christ. For he who lacks these things is shortsighted, even to blindness, and has forgotten that he was cleansed from his old sins. Therefore, brethren, be even more diligent to make your call and election sure, for if you do these things you will never stumble; for so an entrance will be supplied to you abundantly into the everlasting kingdom of our Lord and Savior Jesus Christ (2 Peter 1:5-11).

Those most prone to walk in duplicity in their life are those who refuse to be proactive in their daily faith walk. We must understand that there is no middle ground or neutrality in the Spirit. We are either going forward or backward. And if we are going backward, how long does it take to recover those steps in order to move forward once again?

Luke records the story of the rich young ruler, exposing the plight of those with "too many minds." He approached Jesus, wanting to know how he can get in on this great deal being offered of "eternal life". "Now a certain ruler asked Him, 'Good Teacher, what shall I do to inherit eternal life?'" (Luke 18:18). Jesus told him to keep the commandments. The young ruler assured Jesus he had been diligent to keep the commandments since he was a youth. "What more do I lack?"

Luke gives us a poignant scene that follows. "When Jesus heard these things, He said to him, 'You still lack one thing. Sell all that you have and distribute to the poor, and you will have treasure in heaven; and come follow Me'" (Luke 18:22).

Never get into the game, "Can You Top This?" with Jesus. He will always look past the surface issues to the heart of the matter. Jesus discerned that this rich young man did not lack sincerity. But sincerity was not enough. He must be willing to loose himself from his "double-minded" position. His riches were an ensnarement to his ability to wholeheartedly follow the Master. Thus his decision proved what Jesus already knew: "When he heard this, he became very sorrowful, for he was very rich" (Luke 18:23). No, it was not the riches that he held. It was the riches that held him. Jesus did not want his riches. He wanted him.

Some of the profound, enduring examples of those who were liberated from their wealth into a true life of freedom have been recorded for us in Church history. A spiritual legacy of church buildings, orphanages, schools, and hospitals has been left behind. Why? Because they did not debate the request of Jesus, "Go and sell what you have, give it to the poor. And come follow Me." They simply obeyed out of love and devotion for Him. They counted the cost and the privilege of having Jesus Christ alone as their true treasure, knowing that all the riches and knowledge of God are found in Him. Their names are as fragrant today as the day they were recorded in the annuls of church history — Francis Assisi, Ignatius of Loyola, Madame Guyon, Count Zinzendorf, William Borden, and John G. Lake, just to name a few of God's rare gems. These gave up all to follow Him wholeheartedly and confessed gladly, as the psalmist did, that the LORD was their portion. They removed the danger of being "scattered" in soul or having "too many minds". And they were anointed with power, being given "the mind of Christ" and were rewarded with the riches of heaven.

In the end only one thing is needful: The choice to follow one Master, the Lord Jesus Christ. He challenges each who would follow Him: "For what will it profit a man if he gains the whole world and loses his own soul?" (Mark 8:36).

Paul, discerning where his true treasure lay wrote these words:

> Not that I have already attained, or am already perfected; but I press on, that I may lay hold of that for which Christ Jesus has also laid hold of me. Brethren, I do not count myself to have apprehended; but one thing I do, forgetting those things which are behind and reaching forward to those things which are ahead, I press toward the goal for the prize of the upward call of God in Christ Jesus (Philippians 3:12-14).

I'm sure in the light of eternity Paul had the right focus.

# The Restored SOUL

## Chapter Five

*The LORD is my shepherd; I shall not want.*
*He makes me to lie down in green pastures;*
*He leads me beside the still waters.*
*He restores my soul;*
*He leads me in the paths of righteousness*
*For His name's sake.*
(Psalm 23:1-3)

What prompted her to make an appointment to see me is still somewhat of a mystery to me. But after meeting with this dear lady, I was convinced that the only real explanation for her coming to my office was the Lord.

As she sat across from my desk, she blurted out, "I don't know why I've come here today." I waited... giving her time to compose her thoughts. She began to tell me her story, kind of wandering all over the map of her life, as it were. I listened patiently as she told of her divorce and subsequently how her children, who were grown, did not want anything to do with her. A friend had invited her to our church services a few weeks prior to our visit. She reluctantly came, "for the sake of my friend". She went on to say, "I don't like this church. I don't like the music. I didn't want to come back. But I did." I simply smiled, thinking to myself, "Well, at least she is being brutally honest."

Then she doubled back to why she wanted to talk to me. She had come one Sunday morning and had heard me speak on, "God can give us beauty for ashes."

"This had struck a nerve in me," she explained. She shared a little bit more of her disillusionment with life. Then, finally, she had finished telling me her story.

While I sat listening to this dear lady, I felt a deep sense of compassion for her. She obviously had experienced one disappointment after another. Nothing seemed to be going right in her life. She had almost become hardened through bitterness, hopelessness and despair. Could anything ever change? In fact, the deeper question she intimated was, "Does God even care about me? Am I beyond His help?" This was the real reason she was in my office. She had lost her way and was looking for answers. She was holding onto one last thread of hope that her life still had meaning.

I knew that if she could trust again, all was not lost and beyond God's repair. Therefore I asked her, "Do you want to be healed of your hurt?"

She looked up at me as if I were a Martian from outer space. "Yes, of course!" she exclaimed.

I then had her write down in her notebook all the names of the people who had in some way betrayed her trust or hurt or disappointed her. I waited while she did this.

Next, I asked, "Would you be willing to forgive all of these people you've listed, even God, who you feel is partially to blame for your present circumstances?" There was silence. She froze, folded her arms and stared blankly into space for a few seconds. Finally she commented, "I can try to forgive these people; but God... I'm not so sure I can forgive." I explained the biblical importance of forgiving others, and the consequences of walking in unforgiveness; that it was like putting people in prison, as well as oneself, and then throwing away the key!

She wanted to think about it.

I made no follow-up appointment, but over the next few Sundays, whom did I see at the prayer rail during service time? This dear lady! On one occasion after praying at the altar rail, she deliberately came over to the section where I was standing, looked up at me and smiled before heading back to her seat. I could tell that something had changed. Her entire countenance was all aglow!

It was not long after, that this dear lady, who "did not like our services or the music", began attending the mid-week service as well! Not only attend but also she entered into the celebration in all its aspects! Over the next few months, I witnessed such a transformation you could not recognize her as the same lady who came into my office full of bitterness, hopelessness and despair. She no longer isolated herself but boldly joined the women's group and became a volunteer, joyfully serving in whatever way she could. And I marveled at what a natural soul winner she was; reaching out fearlessly to the hurting and the lost with the hope and love of Jesus Christ.

What had happened to bring about such a radical change? When she made the decision to forgive, she began to regain control of her life; she no longer was a prisoner in her own house. Suddenly, she found a reason to live, and her life took on purpose and significance. God in His faithfulness and infinite mercy began a new work that restored her soul.

Until the soul is restored by God, it is like a house without doors or a fortress without gates. Nehemiah is a great example of one whom God used to help His people rebuild and restore the walls of their city. He understood that the re-hanging of the gates was the first step in helping the people regain the security and dignity God intended for their lives.

Likewise, until the spiritual gates are restored in our lives, we are easy prey for the attacks of the enemy of our soul. Peter warns us that we are to "Be sober, be vigilant; because your adversary the devil walks about like a roaring lion, seeking whom he may devour. Resist him, steadfast in the faith..." (1 Peter 5:8-9). When gates are properly hung, they can keep out intruders and also control who or what comes in.

In the Book of Nehemiah, chapter three, we have the story of the re-hanging of the gates. The order and sequence of the hanging of each gate is suggestive, spiritually, of the way in which the Holy Spirit helps to replace gates in our life. In this way God assists in restoring the soul as it was intended to be—a witness to His grace and glory in our life.

**The Sheep Gate**
The "Sheep Gate" is the first gate Nehemiah helped restore. This gate is suggestive of the way of salvation. Jesus said that He was the Gate, or the Door, of the Sheepfold. No one can come to God but through Him. He announces to each of us that He is the Way, the Truth, and the Life (John

10:1-10; John 14:6). Again, we are reminded by Isaiah, "All we like sheep have gone astray; we have turned, every one, to his own way; and the LORD has laid the iniquity of us all upon Him" (Isaiah 53:6). There is no hope of recovering our true selves unless we come to the Gate of Salvation, which is Jesus Christ.

**The Fish Gate**
The "Fish Gate" is the next gate Nehemiah helps to restore. This is suggestive of the gate of the soul winner. We recall that Jesus found His first disciples while they were still in fishing boats. He said, "Follow Me and I will make you fishers of men." They immediately obeyed and began to follow Him. As He taught them through His words and deeds, they were given the training and the tools necessary to win people to Jesus Christ. It is not always easy to win people to the Master. It takes spiritual skills. The scriptures teach, "He that wins souls is wise" (Proverbs 11:30). Only through God's grace, wisdom and love are people drawn to Him with a desire to give their whole life and allegiance to Him. But our Lord promised, "No one can come to Me unless the Father who sent Me draws him" (John 6:44).

**The Old Gate**
The "Old Gate" is the next gate repaired. This is suggestive to me of Transformation. Paul said, "If anyone is in Christ, he is a new creation; old things have passed away; behold all things have become new" (2 Corinthians 5:17). The "old" is the former manner of life. The "new" is the new person we have become by virtue of Jesus living on the inside of us. When God makes our life new, it will be manifest by a

whole new way of living. We do not have to live the way we formerly lived, in bondage or defeat. The Holy Spirit is alive inside of us to bring forth the God-kind of fruit, which is, "Love, joy, peace, longsuffering, kindness, goodness, faithfulness, gentleness, and self-control" (Galatians 5:22-23).

**The Valley Gate**
The "Valley Gate" is the next gate. Valleys in the scriptures are often a picture of those places where we face trials, tests or other difficulties along the Christian way. It is often in the midst of adversity that we learn how to lean more trustingly upon our Shepherd, the Lord Jesus. David wrote, "Yea, though I walk through the valley of the shadow of death... for You are with me... Your rod and your staff, they comfort me" (Psalm 23:4). We are never to be defeated or discouraged in the midst of trials. Rather through faith, we can turn our trials into places of triumph. God has promised to turn "the Valley of Baca (Weeping) into springs" (Psalm 84:6). Tests come to us not to break us but to make us stronger in the Lord.

**The Refuse Gate**
The Valley Gate leads us on to the "Refuse Gate". This is the gate where the trash was carried out of the city. I call this "The Place of Letting Go": letting go of people, places and things that are no longer a part of our life in God. Paul wrote, "What things were gain to me, these I have counted loss for Christ. Yet indeed I also count all things loss for the excellence of the knowledge of Christ Jesus my Lord, for whom I have suffered the loss of all things, and count them as rubbish, that I may gain Christ" (Philippians 3:7-8).

It is often after great trials that we re-assess what is truly important and beneficial in our life. Then we cast off or, as it were, throw away those things. Paul recognized that the good things were keeping him from the best in God. He recognized as Jim Elliot, a missionary martyred in Equador by the Auca Indians, wrote, "He is no fool who loses what he cannot gain, to gain what he cannot lose."

### The Fountain Gate

From there we come to the "Fountain Gate". This is the gate of renewal and refreshing. Jesus invites all who are thirsty to come to Him and freely drink. Out of their innermost beings "would flow rivers of living water" (John 7:38). The deeper we fall in love with Jesus, the more He fills our life to overflowing with the Holy Spirit. This is evident by a greater manifestation of His love flowing from us to others. Paul said, "The love of God has been poured out in our hearts by the Holy Spirit" (Romans 5:5).

### The Water Gate

Next is the "Water Gate". This is the place of sanctification and cleansing. The Water Gate was the place where Ezra, a teaching priest, gathered the people to hear and learn of the Word of God. The people were so filled with joy that they wept as they heard God's Word. The Word of God is vitally important in shaping our lives into a holy people. Jesus prayed, "Father, sanctify them by Your truth. Your Word is Truth" (John 17:17). Again, Paul wrote of Jesus' Bride, "cleanse her with the washing of the water by the Word" (Ephesians 5:26-27). May we never take for granted the Word of God.

## The Horse Gate

The "Horse Gate" was the next gate to be repaired. The horse has ever been a symbol of conquest and triumph. It speaks to us of the Place of Conquest, or the Place of the Conqueror. You will remember that eight times in the Book of the Revelation there is an announcement of rewards for those "who overcome". God wants you to know that you are an overcomer, not an under-achiever! He wants you to know, "He who is in you is greater than he that is in the world" (1 John 4:4). Again, Paul reminds us that, "Yet in all these things we are more than conquerors through Him who loved us" (Romans 8:37).

## The East Gate

The ninth gate is the "East Gate". The East Gate is the gate for the entrance of the King. It is the gate of His appearing. God's people are to have an eager expectation of the Lord's coming for His people. Jesus said we are to "Watch therefore, for you do not know the hour your Lord is coming" (Matthew 24:42).

We read in Hebrews, "Christ was offered once to bear the sins of many. To those who eagerly wait for Him, He will appear a second time, apart from sin, for salvation" (Hebrews 9:28).

Again, angels appeared from heaven to assure the first apostles that Jesus whom they had seen ascend up in the clouds would one day come back in clouds (Acts 1:11). Lift up your heart, His coming draws near!

## The Inspection Gate

Finally, there was the "Miphkad Gate", or the "Inspection

Gate". It reminds us of the fact that the great day of Judgment is drawing near, when each of us will face the King of kings and Judge of all judges.

Sinners, those who have not accepted God through Jesus Christ as Savior, will stand before the Great White Throne Judgment. They will give account of the deeds done in the body, what they've done in this life, good or evil. Again, Paul tells us that the believers, those who have put their faith in God through Jesus Christ as their Savior, will stand before the Judgment Seat of Christ. They will receive or lose their reward according to the manner of work they did for Him after salvation.

Paul said, "Our work will be tested by fire." If our work is "wood, hay or stubble", there will be loss—no reward, albeit they will be saved. For others, if their work is "gold, silver, precious stones", the fire will test it and their work will remain (1 Corinthians 3:10-15). They shall receive robes and crowns in recognition of their love and service for Him.

You may ask, "How will we know if our work is wood, hay, and stubble or gold, silver, and precious stones?" My friend and mentor, Leonard Ravenhill, once put it this way, "Wood, hay and stubble is that which can be seen above the ground. But gold, silver, precious stones are those things which are hidden beneath the ground." In other words, we do our works not to be seen by men but only for the eyes of God. If our motive is love for Him, we shall not lose our reward, even if you do something as small as giving a cup of cold water in the name of the Lord (Matthew 10:42; Mark 9:41).

This is the hour when we must make sure that every gate is securely hung in our life. In this way, we are assured of fully recovering our true soul's identity and destiny. We must stay upon the Wall of Faith until the work is done, "being confident of this very thing, that He who begun a good work in you will complete it until the day of Jesus Christ" (Philippians 1:6).

We must no longer live merely for the things of time. But let us live in the light of eternity. Time is short. Eternity will last forever.

# The Prayerful SOUL

## Chapter Six

*Now in the morning, having risen a long while before daylight, [Jesus] went out and departed to a solitary place; and there he prayed* (Mark 1:35).

I was literally dumbfounded by what I heard. My wife, Deede, who knows me best, sensed that my mind and emotions were reeling at that moment. She gently and imperceptibly reached over and placed a calming hand upon my arm. Had she not done so, I'm not sure I would not have politely excused myself and left the room. What was it that stunned me so?

I had just been asked to consider taking on a church staff role as "Pastor of Prayer". I smile now as I recall this story, for in that moment, becoming a prayer pastor was the furthest thought from my mind. Little did I know that it would be one of the greatest blessings and privileges God has ever given me.

Please don't misunderstand. I love prayer and have been a faithful practitioner for all thirty years of my Christian experience. It has been my joy to pray with (and for) people all over the world, with many outstanding answers to prayer. At this particular time, if anyone had told me God was birthing a Prayer Movement across the nation and around the world, I would have been hard pressed to believe it. I had traveled from one end of the country to the other for nearly seven years, speaking and teaching in a variety of Christian gatherings. Only twice was I invited to participate in a regularly scheduled "prayer meeting". This was different! I was being given a unique opportunity to participate in that which was closest to the heart of Jesus. Thankfully, God gave me the grace to say, "Yes, I will do it."

Over the next seven years, as Pastor of Prayer and Spiritual Renewal, I had the privilege, joy and honor of praying with and leading others in prayer, the "art of the heart". Prayer became my mission and passion.

Prayer is one of the greatest points of fellowship with our Lord Jesus. He prayed regularly, faithfully and fervently to accomplish the will of God in the earth. He now reigns in heaven where "He always lives to make intercession for us" (Hebrews 7:25). As Leonard Ravenhill said, "Prayer is omnipotent—all powerful. It can do anything that God can do." And again he said, "Prayer is omnipresent. It can go anywhere God can go." If that is so, why don't more people pray? Why is there such lack of prayer among God's people? Especially when Jesus announced, "My house shall be a house of Prayer for all nations" (Mark 11:17).

Apart from the lack of priority, I believe the number one reason people do not pray regularly, is their lack of confidence that prayer makes a difference. Prayer is supernatural. You must believe that there is Someone on the other end listening to what is being prayed. Apart from "saying prayers," whether freely spoken or "scripted", there must be confidence that the prayers offered will be answered. Lack of faith that our prayers matter in the whole scheme of things in our world is a reason for the lack of prayer.

### Praying With Others

Taking my new assignment seriously, the first thing I introduced was a "Corporate Prayer Meeting." An invitation was given to come together as the people of God to pray one night a week. We chose a night that was not in conflict with other regular weekly church activities. Some were skeptical that people would attend. But, lo and behold! From the very first meeting, people came even though the meetings lasted two hours.

People from every type of Christian background came. Some liked to pray out loud, and some prayed quietly. Some liked to kneel and pray, and some preferred to walk and pray. It was wonderful!

How were we able to "pull off" a prayer meeting with such diversity? Simple! In leading the meeting, I reminded everyone, "God is delighted when we come together to pray. He is honored when we maintain unity in the midst of diversity." Finally, I would comment, "We are not here to compete or compare our 'prayer-styles,' but we are here to bring glory and honor to God."

Somehow, in God's mercy and designated leadership, it worked. Not only did God honor our efforts, but that prayer meeting continues to this day, even as I am writing. Many blessings have resulted in answer to the prayers offered to God during these blessed times.

We did not use this prayer time as merely an occasion to pray over a "list of prayers". There were other opportunities for people to pray over lists. This meeting would be a meeting of the heart, seeking God as to what was on His heart without our agenda getting in the way. We opened with a time of worship and asked the Lord, as we waited in His presence, "Lord, would you please give us your heart?" This was by no means "spooky" or "super spiritual". We explained to people that God's will is revealed in His Word. We would seek His heart from the Scriptures, and then pray the Scriptures and promises back to Him. In this way, our prayer times were never boring nor predictable.

We were often emboldened to pray for big matters as well, knowing that His Word does not return void. His Word will accomplish what He sends it to do (Isaiah 55:10-11). We prayed for the needs of the local congregation, but our hearts were enlarged for other peoples and other regions. For example, sometimes we sensed we were to pray for our city, nation, or other nations, and so forth.

Everyone had an opportunity to pray individually, and we grew stronger in prayer together. Some who attended faithfully for months without ever praying openly, would suddenly find their voice, with a release and faith to pray for situations God had impressed upon their heart. Often a few days or weeks later, we would hear how God had answered their petitions.

God loves to answer the prayers of His people. He said, "Call to Me and I will answer you, and show you great and mighty things, which you do not know" (Jeremiah 33:3). Again, John assures us, "Now this is the confidence that we have in Him, that if we ask anything according to His will,

He hears us. And if we know that He hears us, whatever we ask, we know that we have the petitions that we ask of Him" (1 John 5:14-15).

**Personal Prayer**
In addition to corporate prayer, we learned how to have a deeper, ongoing, personal prayer life. I am often asked, "How can I develop a greater personal prayer life?" My initial response is a simple one: "Time and a place."

Establish a meeting place with God. Jesus sets the example in the Gospels. He was up "a great while before day" (Mark 1:35). Even after a long day of ministry, He still rose and sought a solitary place to commune with His heavenly Father. This was an established routine in his life and ministry. The prayerful soul has fixed times and a sacred, or dedicated, place to be alone with God. Solitude helps us empty ourselves of unnecessary clutter of mind and heart to enter into the stillness of God's heart and mind.

Don't try to pray like someone else. No two people pray exactly the same. This is important if we are to achieve consistency in prayer. You are unique. Find out what is your personal "prayer temperament". Your prayer temperament is the way you connect with God in prayer, which overflows and affects your daily life.

Sometimes biblical characters are helpful types or pictures in discovering our prayer style. This has been an understood and accepted norm throughout Church history. I would like to suggest four prayer temperaments, with the understanding that we could possibly find our prayer temperaments changing as we grow and develop in the Lord. The characters I will use to suggest different temperaments are from the Gospels: Martha, Mary, Lazarus and the Lord Jesus.

Martha, the sister of Mary, represents the "active life". Every time you find her in the Scriptures she is very busy, always "up and doing". Some find it hard to stay put; they cannot seem to sit still for a moment. They are quite often that way in prayer. They may not pray well in the quiet, meditative position such as kneeling or sitting. They often find long prayer times intolerable, although this may change over time. For the "Martha" types, prayer through activity when offered to God as sacrament may be a great way to stay connected to God. In other words, taking God into the activity or routine of the day makes a prayerful soul aware that God is in him and in the business at hand.

Mary, the sister of Martha, represents the "contemplative life." She is portrayed in the Gospel as very much a mystic. She is seen sitting in loving silence at the feet of Jesus, listening for His word. For her, solitude and silence is as natural a prayer posture as a sea otter floating on his back while eating a fish. Again, her personal prayer is more about being attentive in His presence, watching with the "eyes of her heart" for the Lover of her soul. She mirrors the words of the psalmist David, "Truly my soul silently waits for God; from Him comes my salvation" (Psalm 62:1).

For the prayerful soul like "Mary", much of prayer is an intuitive experience, a knowing beyond words. It is rather a knowing of hearts, as friend to friend, or lover to the Beloved. She is not inactive, as some "Marthas" would have us believe. Rather, she does not move out quickly from her place of seclusion to activity until she has heard a Word of instruction from His lips. Perhaps this temperament could best be summed up in the words given in a commercial by the late Orson Wells, "There will be no wine before the time."

Very few take into account Lazarus as a type. But to me, he represents a rare prayer temperament. He would be more of the "recluse," not only solitary but also silent. No words are recorded to express his personal trust in God.

Three movements are recorded in scriptures regarding Lazarus. First, there is the movement of love and friendship. Jesus is welcomed into his home and that of Martha and Mary. Second, his sickness that leads to death, which will have only temporary claim on its victim. Then finally, a resurrection scene! Because of Lazarus, many who did not believe "went away and believed in Jesus" (John 12:11).

In some ways, I think Lazarus is a model of those experiencing what St. John of the Cross calls, "The dark night of the soul." It is the prayer of negation, where everything that is done must be done by God. There is nothing in the time of trial that the prayerful soul can do, but be still and know that God is God; and He will be exalted among the nations, He will be exalted in the earth (Psalm 46:10).

"Lazarus" types are in short supply. They are rare souls, who live a life of surrender to what Jean Pierre De Caussade calls "abandonment to Divine providence". This is not fatalism. It is not saying, "Whatever will be, will be." It is rather faithfulness in the midst of seeming contradictions; knowing that, in the end all will be well, because this has happened for the glory of God.

But for most of us, we are neither Martha the active life, nor Mary, the contemplative life, nor like Lazarus the surrendered life. Rather, for the most part, we are called to live the example of our Lord Jesus, whose earthly pattern was the "mixed life".

Jesus lived a balanced life of prayer and service. His entire nights of prayer prepared him for His full days of ministry. His prayer time with the Father was in order to stay attached to His Father, getting His will for the day's challenges that lay ahead.

If we are honest, most of us struggle to find the proper balance between family, work, ministry, and rest. All of these are good and necessary. Living a life of prayer helps to synthesize these priorities in our everyday, work-a-day world.

Taking prayer into your day is a sure way to stay attached to God and to be attentive to His work in your life and the world around you. In this way, you will be able to respond to those moments as God moments with faithfulness, courage, love, joy, and peace. In this way we learn to breathe the famous prayer of Reinhold Niebuhr,

*God, give us grace*
*To accept with serenity*
*The things that cannot be changed,*
*Courage to change the things*
*That should be changed,*
*And the wisdom to distinguish*
*The one from the other.*
Amen.

# *The Awakened* SOUL

## Chapter Seven

*But when it pleased God, who separated me from my mother's womb, and called me through His grace, to reveal his Son in me, that I might preach him among the Gentiles, I did not immediately confer with flesh and blood, nor did I go up to Jerusalem to those who were apostles before me; but I went to Arabia, and returned again unto Damascus* (Galatians 1:15-17).

To a certain degree, we all are shaped by the cultural norms and values in which we are born. This may be a good thing, or it may be a hard shell we have to break out of in order to find our own identity and purpose.

For the most part, my upbringing was a good "incubator" for life. I was born in the city of Detroit and lived within four walls of concrete, which was my childhood impression of city life around me. At the age of ten, I along with my parents, brother and two sisters moved to Georgia where I lived among four walls of trees, pine trees. In both places, our family regularly attended church.

Attending church was a good thing. We children were taken to Sunday school, and afterward joined our parents in the main service. At that time, there was no such thing as "children's church." We children learned how not to squirm and wiggle while the grown-ups "had church". I cannot remember a time as a boy when I did not enjoy good preaching. I recall Reverend Abrams, the Baptist pastor in Detroit, who preached with great eloquence and fervor. Then there was Reverend McMillan, the Methodist pastor in Georgia where we attended, who preached with equal fervor and passion. It was quite typical to both see and hear the folks getting spiritually and emotionally worked up by the sermon. I remember these boyhood times with great fondness.

I discovered, however, that just because people were regular Sunday church attendees and loved to hear good preaching, they did not always apply it during the rest of the week. In my youthful innocence, I became aware of "dual lifestyles"— gossip, drunkenness, domestic violence, abuse, and whispers of adulterous affairs among some of these fine church folk. This for me was not a good thing.

As I grew older, I became thoroughly disillusioned with the "church." I do not say I knew God personally at that time, but in the inner core of my being, I truly longed to know Him. Hypocritical living almost drove me away from the "organized" church. Parents and adults do not realize the impact their example can make on young, impressionable children—for better or worse. Children learn what they see and hear.

But in the midst of my disillusionment, I was ambushed by God. He saw my heart, that I truly wanted to know Jesus Christ as my Savior. In my mind I struggled with whether or not it was possible to find Him in the "church" system in which I had grown up. God, who knew me better than I knew Him, had mercy on me.

While at this crisis juncture in my life, I decided to "Join the Navy and See the World". And right on the heels of this momentous decision, I hit another crisis. I went through an unexpected breakup with the girl I thought I was going to marry. This shattered my world; all my little plans seemed to fall around me in a thousand pieces. God, who I was convinced was a shameless opportunist, took this occasion to pry open the door of my heart, breaking in with His light and love into a poor, dark soul. Two weeks before I was to report for military basic training, I knelt at my bedside and surrendered my life, hopes and dreams into the hands of Jesus Christ, whatever that future may mean.

I wish I could say like some that, "I heard the birds begin to sing, and the grass appeared greener, and the sky became bluer." Nothing like that happened to me. There was simply a settled knowing that, for the first time, my life belonged to God. During the next few months, I completed my training and graduated from Hospital Corpsmen Training School. Then, I was unexpectedly stationed aboard a naval vessel. It was at this new juncture that an awareness of a spiritual awakening took place in my soul.

I was assigned to the USS-Dixie AD-14, affectionately called by the crew, "USS-Dixie Never-Sail." She was the oldest U.S. Navy ship in commission! She was a Destroyer Tender, assigned to take care of Navy Aircraft Carriers. Aboard this vessel, I made a commitment to rise before breakfast and spend some time with God in prayer and His Word.

Through the grace of God, I began to keep my appointment with Him. I would go into the little medical office and shut myself in with God and His Word. I enjoyed these times alone with God and somehow had a strange awareness that He enjoyed them too. What I didn't know at the time was how much the Word and prayer were changing me from inside out.

Then it happened!

A big verbal row broke out among the other medical corpsmen in our department because "an order" had been given to strip a floor and replace it with brand new tile. The problem sparking the row was the fact that the floor was perfectly fine, and we were being given "busy work". The medical crew knew it and resented it. In addition to this added chore, it cut in on the "free time" afforded the sailors while docked in port. Were they ever steamed and worked up over this! Shouts and "sailor language" were flying everywhere.

One of the corpsmen, who was senior to me in rank, was not only angry over the situation but turned his verbal aggression on me. He could not understand why I had not joined them in this verbal "mutiny" in expressing displeasure over our unfortunate and unhappy circumstance. The truth is that it did not occur to me at that moment to do so. And besides, I figured it would not change anything... "AN ORDER WAS AN ORDER" to be obeyed, not debated. Therefore, my peaceful composure only exacerbated the feelings of this one corpsman.

Turning on me, like a raccoon treed by a hound dog, he got right up in my face and shouted glaringly, "Why aren't you saying something?!!!" At that moment, I was overwhelmed with a sense of the peace of God. I had never experienced anything like this before. Please understand, it would not have been my response prior to giving my life to God! If someone had been in my face like this previously, it would have provoked a sure physical confrontation. But in that moment, I was enveloped by God's love. I felt the Spirit of the Lord whisper to my heart, "Hold your peace. Don't say anything." Then after a few awkward seconds, the senior corpsman backed down and turned away. He was still frustrated and perplexed, as if he saw something in my eyes, and said no more. In that moment, something else miraculous happened. I watched the entire group grow quiet as well. For me it was an epiphany—a conscious awakening within my soul. I knew that the Lord had taken control of the situation. And more than that, I knew He had taken control of me in a way that was previously unknown.

Although I had no doubt that I had given my life completely over to His Lordship, I had been still battling with anger inside from issues in my youth. But in that instant, I realized Jesus had swept it all away! I have never felt anger that made me feel out of control again. What had happened? God had flushed all the anger, resentment, and bitterness from my past away, and had replaced it with His grace, peace and self-control. I was free!

Paul must have known something of the reality of this process of his soul's awakening to spiritual reality. He apparently had a high rank among the Sanhedrin, the Ultra-Jewish religious sect of his day, and was well on his way to making quite a name for himself. If they had a "Who's Who" among the Jews in that era, his name, Saul of Tarsus, would have been among them. He thought his way was right and anybody that challenged that would be in for a sure fight.

But one day he had an experience that forever altered his religious course and career.

A new religious sect had emerged in Jerusalem, known as "The Way". They were disciples of Jesus of Nazareth, whom Pilate had crucified. They claimed He had been raised from the dead. This infuriated Saul of Tarsus. He commenced and personally led a vigorous campaign to exterminate this new movement. He authorized the relentless persecution of the followers of Jesus. Some he arrested, others he had beaten and jailed. He even gave his personal consent to the murder of Stephen, the first martyr of the Church (Acts 8). And then one day it happened.

Saul was on his way to Damascus, with legal papers in hand to expand the territory of his zealous, murderous persecution of the believers, when he was suddenly struck blind! (Acts 9). He heard a voice call him by name saying, "Saul, Saul. Why are you persecuting me?" When he asked "Who are you, Lord?" what he heard did not leave him just physically blind, but flattened spiritually as well. "I am Jesus whom you are persecuting" was the Lord's reply (Acts 9:5).

Saul was led into the city of Damascus, where he stayed for the next three days, eating nothing. I have a sneaking suspicion he slept poorly as well. He pondered what had happened to him. The physical blindness caused a slow but steady spiritual dawning of the reality that Jesus of Nazareth was indeed the long awaited Messiah! Saul suddenly realized that, in his religious zeal "for God", he had actually become an enemy of God. Further still, the people for whom he had such a hatred were, in fact, part of the family of God! Not only were they family, they were part of the Body of Messiah (Christ). As a result of this revelation, his heart was broken. Saul repented of his spiritual blindness, and God restored his physical sight. And Saul became Paul an apostle to the Gentiles.

How often our preconceived ideas and prejudices, even those which may have been theological positions, have left us, as it were, blind to the light of God's truth He longed to reveal to us. Like Paul, we might have, in ignorance, found ourselves closed to God's further plans and purposes for our life. It takes great humility and honesty to stay open and teachable. Jesus told his disciples there would be more to come. "I have much more to say to you," He said. "But you are not ready to receive it. But when He the Spirit of Truth comes, He will take the things which are Mine and reveal them to you" (John 16:12-15).

This awakening for Paul on the road to Damascus was apparently just one of a series of "awakenings" to his soul by the Lord Jesus. He writes of his experience to the Galatians, "When it pleased the Lord... to reveal His Son in me" (Galatians 1:12). It seems that Paul is referring to more than a revelation of the Lord Jesus to him on the Damascus road. Perhaps he is referring to his experience while sequestered in study and reflection of the scriptures in the Arabian Desert. Wherever it took place, a greater revelation of Jesus Christ gave a deeper, inward knowledge of Him to Paul's soul as well.

We too, in the course of our journeying with the Lord Jesus, will experience a greater measure of inward grace and knowledge. This, I believe, is implied in the invitation of our Lord Jesus who said, "Come unto Me all you who labor and are heavy laden, and I will give you rest. Take My yoke upon you and learn of Me, for I am gentle and lowly in heart, and you will find rest for your souls" (Matthew 11:27-28).

Please notice that Jesus offers those that come to Him the possibility of two kinds of "rest." First, in our initial response of faith to Jesus Christ, He brings our spirit His peace and rest. Paul wrote, "Therefore being justified by faith we have peace with God through our Lord Jesus Christ" (Romans 5:1). But, Jesus goes on to say that those who take on His yoke will find "rest for their soul". This is a greater dimension of rest.

Our souls find rest when we have surrendered to the yoke of His Lordship, being conformed to His will and ways in our life. The writer to the Hebrew Christians exhorts them to cling wholeheartedly to Jesus as the "Captain of their salvation," knowing that He is able to complete in them what he has begun, "the saving of the soul" (Hebrews 10:39).

There are dimensions in the soul of each individual, in other words, our mind, will, emotions and choices that God desires to shape until we are conformed to the image of His Son, Jesus Christ. He is able to achieve this by our faith, cooperation and obedience to the Holy Spirit's direction, and conformity to the Word of God. This is what it means to be "yoked up" with Jesus. His yoke is a yoke of fellowship, learning to know His heartbeat and discerning His ways and will. Again, it is a yoke of discipline, learning what it means to be a true disciple of Jesus.

A disciple is a student apprentice who learns from the Master-Teacher with the understanding that one day he will be and do what the Master says and does. Finally, it is a yoke of partnership, learning to follow His lead, cooperating in His purposes in order to bring forth fruit to the glory of God the Father. Paul wrote, "As many as are led by the Spirit of God are the sons of God" (Romans 8:14). Again, "We are His workmanship, created in Christ Jesus for good works" (Ephesians 2:10).

G. Campbell Morgan, gifted preacher and teacher in the early 1900s, once observed, "As Christians we are called to be more than just good. We are called to be good for something!"

Taking on the yoke of Jesus is a voluntary commitment of love and devotion to Him. Jesus did the same, as an example for you and me, in relation to His heavenly Father. While He walked and worked among us, He bore the yoke of love and obedience. He said to His Father, "Not my will but Thy will be done" (Matthew 26:39). Only those who long for a greater awakening within their soul will take upon them His yoke. He promises that His yoke is easy and His burden is light (Matthew 11:30). Only those who bear His yoke will know the joy and satisfaction of resting in Him. The writer to the Hebrews assures us, "For he who has entered His rest has himself also ceased from his works as God did from His" (Hebrews 4:10). Corrie Ten Boom reminded us, "Don't wrestle… nestle!"

*You look around and you're distressed;*
*You look within and you're depressed;*
*But look to Him and you're at rest!*
Corrie Ten Boom

# *The Worshipful* SOUL

## Chapter Eight

*My soul magnifies the Lord, and my spirit does rejoice in God my Savior* (Luke 1:46).

*Jesus answered him, "The first of all the commandments is: Hear, O Israel, the LORD our God, the LORD is one. And you shall love the LORD your God with all your heart, with all your soul, with all your mind, and with all your strength. This is the first commandment"* (Mark 12:29-30).

I had not planned this on my calendar. It just sort of worked out that because of my citywide ministry involvement, I was invited to be a part of three different and distinct Christian gatherings in less than thirty-six hours. One of those would be held in a home not far from where I live. It was a house church meeting within walking distance in my neighborhood.

When I arrived at the home, the meeting had already started. Music was wafting throughout the room, compliments of a worship CD. Most of the people attending were seated with faces uplifted, eyes closed, quietly singing along with the worship leader on tape. The sense of the presence of the Lord was tangible and genuine. After perhaps fifteen or twenty minutes of music and singing, a guest speaker stood and brought a message from the Word of God. This was followed by a time of personal prayer and ministry to most people present. It was wonderful! I found myself returning home so alive in my spirit that it took me several hours to fall asleep on that Friday night.

Then about thirty-six hours later, I walked into another service. This one was being held in a different part of town in a quaint old building, with beautiful architectural design. It was tastefully done with high ceilings and stained glass window reliefs featuring biblical characters from the Bible. This service was much more structured, but the atmosphere was bright. The great hymns of the church being sung lifted our spirits, directing our thoughts toward God. After singing, we read together aloud various scripture portions. Then we knelt to pray, and sat down. The minister, who is a pastor friend of mine, brought an exceptionally rich message regarding John the Baptist, with personal application to us, the hearers. Afterward, we celebrated the table of the Lord together. This was the highlight and centerpiece of the service. I was conscious of the Lord's presence among us as I joined others who came forward to partake of this spiritual meal together.

From there, I was scheduled to be with another young pastor friend. I have been somewhat of a mentor-friend to him and his congregation. Their services were held in an area of the city where the crime rate and drug activity had been exceedingly high, until they moved into the neighborhood and began holding services. Nothing seen from the outside of the building would attract you to their services. Apart from the address and a simple posted sign on the side of the building, nothing announces their presence in the area. They met in a warehouse building which has been attractively renovated to accommodate those who gather. They are doing an excellent work for the Lord.

When I walked into the building, a young man casually dressed greeted me warmly. In the background, I could hear the quiet hum of the "pre-service" prayer meeting taking place in the main auditorium. No printed programs were handed out. When I stepped into the sanctuary, I noticed the pastor was leading the prayer time. In a few moments, someone else from the congregation approached a microphone and began praying. Others were fervently asking God, "Come and visit this place with Your presence and power," and the Lord heard their prayers.

In a few moments, with the main service beginning, God's presence became evident. A young lady, accompanied by a worship band, stepped up on the platform and started leading the congregation in contemporary worship choruses. The songs were heart-searching and intentionally directed toward intimacy with God. For the next twenty to thirty minutes, the place was filled with joyful voices and a deep awareness of His loving presence. This was followed by the young pastor's inspiring biblical message. He challenged us all to "live more like Jesus" in our everyday affairs. It was a wonderful experience!

My point in sharing my experiences at these three services was to call your attention to the fact that although each was distinct, in a different location, with different styles, I met God in worship. How could it be otherwise when the people had gathered in the name of the Lord for the definite purpose of bringing glory and honor to Him! He said, "Wherever two or three gather together in My name there I am in the midst" (Matthew 18:20). It was neither the place nor the style that attracted the presence of the Lord; rather, it was worship that sanctified the place and satisfied longing hearts with His presence. God comes to hearts that are open and available to the gracious work of His Holy Spirit.

Worship was one of the obvious signs of Abraham's friendship with God. He was known as "a pilgrim and stranger in the land" (Hebrews 11:13). What distinguished his pilgrimage was the "tent and the altar" in his camp. Wherever Abraham journeyed, he pitched his tent and built an altar, sanctifying a space for God to meet with him.

The soul worshiping God enters into the mystery of the design of creation. Nothing really makes sense in the eternal scheme of things until we realize that the ultimate purpose of our existence is to worship. Worship is a cry for intimate knowing. To worship is to acknowledge, in some appropriate way, our thanks and allegiance to the One who is bigger or greater than we are.

Worship begins as gratitude of the heart. It finds its expression of this inward gratitude by an outward act. This is true the world over. The difference for the Christian is that worship is not directed to "something". For, to worship a creature or creation would be idolatry, or to use the description of the Old Testament prophets, spiritual adultery. We are not called to worship "something" but "Someone," namely God, Who has revealed Himself as Creator and Redeemer of all mankind.

When Jesus sat by a well at high noon in Samaria, He did so not merely because He was tired and hungry; He sat down to reveal to thirsty souls the true meaning of their existence. A woman approached the well. Inside of her was a desperate longing to belong to someone, not as an object of lust but as someone who would be loved and cherished for who she was as a person. Jesus knew her better than she knew herself. He knew she had lived with five different men, and the one with her now was the sixth. He knew also that what she really needed was to meet the "Seventh Man" sitting by the well. Seven is a biblical number that represents "completeness". There is none more complete than Jesus Christ.

In the course of their conversation, the Samaritan woman sensed that in Jesus was One who knew her through and through, and yet loved her unconditionally. He wanted nothing from her but water to quench his thirst. She longed for nothing more from Him than a drink that would quench her thirsty soul. He gave her the key—worship.

I can imagine the conversation going something like this: Jesus observing, "What you are missing is the key to intimacy with God, which is worship."

"Worship, Sir?"

"Yes, worship, which is not religiously prescribed to a time or place, but is beyond time and space. Worship is a living reality which flows from a heart of love and devotion to a Person, Father God." Then in the words recorded by John, He says, "The hour is coming, and now is, when the true worshipers will worship the Father in spirit and truth; for the Father is seeking such to worship Him. God is Spirit, and those who worship Him must worship in spirit and truth" (John 4:23-24).

Jesus does not say the Father is recruiting singers for the "heavenly choir" when they die. No, but rather that the Father is seeking those who will join in worship with the heavenly choir, now, while they live here on the earth.

## The Nature of Worship

The worshipful soul knows that true worship is a function of the soul and spirit in response to the Holy Spirit and the Truth of God as revealed in Jesus Christ through His Word. The more we worship the Father by honoring the Son, the more the Holy Spirit lifts and liberates us to become who we have been called to be. This is what the woman at the well discovered. She became the first woman evangelist, bringing hope and the Good News of Jesus Christ to her entire village.

New things are born through worship, as the Virgin Mary exemplifies. After she was visited by the angel Gabriel, she went to visit her cousin Elizabeth. She was so thrilled with God's announcement that she was to bring forth the long awaited Messiah, she broke out into her Magnificat. "My soul magnifies the Lord, and my spirit has rejoiced in God my Savior. For He who is mighty has done great things for me, and holy is His name" (Luke 1:46, 47, 49).

Mary sang this knowing that although she may be a virgin, "nothing is impossible with God" when the Holy Spirit overshadows your life. She worshiped in anticipation of the miraculous birth of our Lord through her womb.

What thing seems impossible or delayed in coming to pass in your life? Is there a promise that seems outstanding that you have claimed from the Word of God? Perhaps the key of worship will bring to birth your miracle. The prophet Isaiah exhorts,

> *Sing, O barren, you who have not borne! Break forth into singing, and cry aloud, you who have not labored with child! For more are the children of the desolate than the children of the married woman, says the LORD* (Isaiah 54:1).

What is the point God is making? When He wants to bring something to birth in our life, it does not depend on our cleverness or human capacity. Worship acknowledges that this must be done by God through the agency of His Word, which Peter describes as "the incorruptible seed of God" (1 Peter 1:23). God's word placed by faith into the "barren womb" of our circumstance will bring forth the desired promises. As Kevin Conner, minister and biblical author, once said, "It takes more faith to sing before the baby is born than after it gets here!"

Worship is an expression of our recognition of the worth of God. This is the reason that in worship we should offer God our best. In other words, the worshipful soul has no problem understanding that God deserves the best we can give. That is why the children of Israel were instructed to offer God "first fruits". It was a token of appreciation for what the Lord had caused to be produced in their fields of harvest. It was an act of worship unto God, that He had first place and deserved the best in all things.

Further, as an expression of God's worthiness (and our worth), He set aside a full day in which He would be honored while His people would be renewed. A day of worship and rest is a clear sign that God's people truly are a worshipping people. That day is called a "Sabbath," and the prophet Isaiah records, you will "call the Sabbath a delight" (Isaiah 58: 13). Again, worship is said to be of such value because it is spiritually transforming, and we should "worship the LORD in the beauty of holiness" (1 Chronicles 16:29).

One of the ways I am personally convinced we have played into the hands of the enemy is by making the way in which we worship a source of division. The Church of Jesus Christ is now 2,000 years old, and yet only 500 of those years (give or take a few years) has she been divided over our worship style—our liturgy. Liturgy in its true essence means "the work of the people". Public worship is not a solo act or a one-person performance. It is a participation of the people of God in acts of reverence, love and awe given as a visible witness to what our hearts can scarcely express toward God.

This is what God intended when He gave Moses the instructions regarding the priesthood. The priests were to wear certain garments when ministering unto the Lord before the people. They were to be adorned in "garments of glory and beauty" (Exodus 28:2). This visible imagery was to be a prophetic and spiritual symbol of the reality that all of God's people, as priests, were to be holy unto the Lord. Peter wrote to the believers, "But you are a chosen generation, a royal priesthood, a holy nation, His own special people, that you may proclaim the praises of Him who called you out of darkness into His marvelous light" (1 Peter 2:9). We are reminded of this fact in the Book of the Revelation where John receives in symbolic form a vision of the Lord Jesus as our great high priest, adorned with a robe that reaches down to His feet. Later, John sees an innumerable company of people in heaven who have been given "white robes" which speaks of "the righteousness of the saints" (Revelation 19:8).

The point is that images and symbolism aid in our understanding and appreciation of spiritual reality. Therefore, today some in the Body of Christ are given to more physical attire to express this reality of their faith than others. No problem, as long as your preference does not become a badge of "greater" spirituality than your lesser adorned brothers. And vice-versa. Those who have a "liberty" not to wear outward adornments, but worship from the heart, know the inward reality of these things. Not wearing ornate adornments does not make one more spiritual or any more "free in the spirit" than those who do. I write this to call the Church to honesty and accountability over that which has divided the Body. I recall a remarkable quote from George Whitefield, the eminent evangelist of the Great Awakening who was used by God to bring the Body of Christ together. He saw one of the greatest revivals that was the result of his evangelistic efforts. He also saw how many Church leaders were divisive and would not recognize their brothers from other churches. Whitefield wrote in his journal words to this effect, "Lord, see how they have torn your seamless garment!"

What Jesus through the blood of His cross has joined together, may we not rend apart. We are the Body of Christ. Our worship should not be used to divide us but rather to unite us more and more unto Him. May we come to appreciate that in the Body. His love in our hearts can melt away the resistant walls of distinctions that really are often preferences due to cultural heritage and history. May our worship be an occasion for the world to witness the resurrected Jesus alive among His people. And may our celebrations be occasions of praise and thanksgiving, rather than blame, unto God; knowing that whatever we do we are to do all to the greater honor and glory of our Lord Jesus Christ. In the words attributed to John Wesley,

*In things essential, Unity.*
*In things non-essential, Liberty.*
*In all things, Charity.*

# The SOUL of Revival

## Chapter Nine

*The poor and needy seek water,*
*But there is none, Their tongues fail for*
*thirst. I, the LORD, will hear them;*
*I, the God of Israel, will not forsake them.*
*I will open rivers in desolate heights,*
*And fountains in the midst of the valleys;*
*I will make the wilderness a pool of water,*
*And the dry land springs of water.*
(Isaiah 41:17-18)

I needed to do something in the form of exercise and as a means of releasing the stress I was under. I had embarked on my masters and doctoral studies. Both at the same time! I was also teaching fifteen hours of courses as dean of a Bible college, not to mention serving as an associate pastor and an elder of our local congregation. What could I do with this demanding (overloaded!) schedule?

Living at that time in beautiful, sunny San Diego, I decided to take up running, really jogging. To make sure I was getting the most out of my exercise, I subscribed to a runner's magazine, knowing that keeping up with the nuances of running for better health would keep me motivated and focused.

Starting any new skill or discipline has a steep learning curve. This was true for me. Although I did run on the track team in high school, my specialty had been the short distance events, which required speed and technique versus endurance. Now I was about to engage in long distance running which required a bit of an adjustment! Being formerly accustomed to using certain muscle groups (plus being out of shape), I may have covered a half-mile in the beginning before my heart and lungs were begging for air. I was determined to stay with it, and after a few weeks I could run several miles without any trouble.

One of the phenomena I had only read about regarding runners was the experience of getting a "runner's high". This is when you are running along, your legs are heavy and maybe your lungs are telling you that it is time to quit. Then, suddenly, instead of collapsing from exhaustion, you push past those feelings and get this magical "second wind". You feel like you could run on forever! As I increased my distances, I experienced this "second wind" many times while running.

Having spent most of my thirty years of ministry studying the nature of true historical revivals, I have come to the conclusion that true revival in the Church is like getting a "second wind." Whether a revival was Reformation, Quaker, Baptist, Great Awakening, Welsh, or Pentecostal/Charismatic, the secret of these great movements was gaining the "second wind" of the Spirit for God's people.

Revivals have often been called The Romantic Period of the Church, because they are extraordinary. They rarely are telegraphed ahead of time, although when they do appear they are broadcast far and wide. Revivals usually start with a "dark" spiritual backdrop, or a dark curtain in a period of history when the Church, at least on a local level, is either an outright scandal to its true proclaimed nature or is altogether ignored by the community around them. Often, a prelude to a mighty outpouring of God's Spirit in power is a sense of great spiritual lack, lethargy and defeat. Sin is rampant not only in society, but also frequently among spiritual leaders and congregants. In this spiritual malaise, very few salvations are recorded in the Church. As a direct result, the community is unaffected or unmoved to shame over the immorality, injustice, or the spiritual poverty and captivity around them. For example, let's take the recorded historic period in England just prior to the revival known as the "Great Awakening".

It has been said that only one percent of the population of England attended any church services, and only about one-third of Parliament, the elected governmental leaders, bothered to show up for public duty. In society, every fifth house was an alehouse or a brothel. Crime and lawlessness were so rampant that no one dared go out on the dark roads at night, lest they be accosted, robbed or murdered by bands of robbers. Such was the spiritually dark atmosphere that pervaded the land. And yet, history records that under the leadership of such men as George Whitefield and John and Charles Wesley, the spiritual tide turned politically, socially, and religiously. These and other men and women like them became known as Methodists and circuit riders. Preachers who rode, indefatigably, on horseback and under all kinds of conditions and adversities from town to town proclaimed the Good News of Jesus Christ. As a result, throughout all England and subsequently across the Atlantic to America, the Church experienced a "second wind". Her soul was revived.

One of the signs of this second wind or renewal within the Church is God finding Himself a yielded vessel, someone who is available to God for His sovereign use. As Matthew Henry, Bible commentator and minister, observed, "God does nothing but that he sets a people praying." Those who are alert to God in prayer usually pick up God's spiritual frequency, as it were, and begin to share in the burden of His heart. Often that burden will produce a message they are compelled to deliver to God's people. The message, in turn, stirs and provokes people to righteousness once again; they are suddenly awakened out of their spiritual indifference and slumber. This deep conviction settles in upon the hearts of the people, and they become aware of their lack of spiritual hunger for the honor of God. Suddenly they acknowledge before Him and one another their lack of compassion for the lost, the broken and the hurting that are all around them.

This message and deep conviction goes deeper still until groups begin to meet to pray and intercede, asking God for His mercy and cleansing, personally and collectively, for His people (Psalm 85). Usually, it is not long before a new movement of passion for God and compassionate concern expressed toward neighbors who are lost, being far away from God, begins.

It is inevitable that these revival movements create machinery and systems to hold and maintain the fruit of what God is doing. Through messages proclaimed, recorded and distributed in pamphlets and books, news of revival goes forth as a new and living seed of truth. In conjunction with the published word, new music is recorded and set forth in psalms, hymns, and new choruses to capture and preserve the truth that God has revealed. The writings and music reflect the culture of the day.

New moves of God are often accompanied by the element of signs and wonders. For some, it will confirm the work is of God. For others, it will create offense and controversy surrounding the new work of God. It will even be opposed at times. Usually the opposition is by the people who experienced the previous move of God! However, where there is God appointed leadership to "test the fruit" of the work, the storm of controversy can be quelled. The new movement is kept on track and advances welcoming God's Spirit on His terms. God never brings revival in a vacuum. He always uses people.

**Moses and Revival**

One of the distinguished biblical examples of a man used by God to bring revival to His people is Moses (Exodus 3-15). In the midst of a horrendously dark backdrop of human suffering, Israel as a nation emerges. Prior to their deliverance, Moses and the nation of Israel were both physically and spiritually captives under the mighty power of the Egyptian empire and Pharaoh.

Moses was miraculously preserved and sequestered from his people's captivity. For the first forty years of his life, he was raised and educated under the very nose of Pharaoh. Later, after killing an Egyptian, he ran away, escaping certain death, and for the next forty years lived on the backside of the desert. Then one day as he was leading his flock near the Mount of God, he encountered a burning bush—all ablaze but not consumed! This phenomenon got Moses' attention... and God got His man for the new assignment, which was one of the preeminent evidences of revival in the annals of history.

Now let us get back to the story. Moses approached the burning bush with enormous curiosity but soon fell under deep conviction. This was no natural phenomenon but a supernatural encounter with the holy God!

Acknowledging the presence of this holy God, he removed his sandals. He received ample assurances that he was dealing with the God of His ancestors—Abraham, Isaac and Jacob. After further proofs, Moses finally relented from all excuses of inadequacy, recognizing that the task of delivering his people was not his alone. He needed only to be willing in faith to walk out his obedience under God's directives. The God Who had been revealed in the flames of a burning bush would put that same flame, as it were, in his being. He would be God's torchbearer for the hour.

Every revival has its torchbearers. The prophets Elijah and John the Baptist were torchbearers, "burning and shining lights" who prepared God's people for their day of deliverance. Others like them followed, becoming burning witnesses to God's inner flame of revival. How does it happen? It is an open secret. Let nature be our classroom for a moment.

Take an ordinary log, place it into a fire and leave it there. It will not be long before you observe that the fire has engulfed the log in its flame. But wait a few moments more and the fire that was once around the log is now inside the log, glowing with red-hot embers. So, too, when we get near the flame of God, choosing to press into His presence, the flame around us will soon be fire inside of us. The writer to the Hebrew Christians assures us that "Our God is a consuming fire" (Hebrews 12:29).

Those who have experienced the flame of God inwardly will understand that the Man and the Message are one and the same. This is the key and the soul of revival.

God never sends His servants ill equipped. Moses was given more than a message, he was sent with "words and signs" (Exodus 4:28). God gives both the message and the method. Both signs and wonders attest to revivals where the Word of God is faithfully proclaimed.

You will recall our Lord Jesus warned His disciples not to run with the message of His Good News "until you be endued with power from on high" (Luke 24:49). Not knowing what to expect, in obedience they waited during the next ten days. When the Holy Spirit came upon them, signs and wonders accompanied the message they delivered. Mark records, "And they went out and preached everywhere, the Lord working with them and confirming the word through the accompanying signs" (Mark 16:20). Words and signs will attend true revival.

Moses could not forget this lesson if he would be a successful deliverer. Human nature being what it is, he may have received a little reminder from God. I can imagine seeing him going to confront the might of Pharaoh's army, and God walking at his side. The conversation probably went something like this: God looks over and says, "Moses."

To which he replies, "Yes, Lord."

A pause... God continues, "Moses, I don't want you to forget the burning bush."

Moses, surprised and perhaps a little incredulous, says, "Oh! LORD, I could never forget the burning bush."

God replies, "Good! As long as you understand that it is you who provides the bush... I provide the flame! By the way, I can use any old shrub yielded to Me. It only takes a spark to get a fire going!"

# *The* SOUL *of the* Church

## Chapter Ten

*So continuing daily with one accord in the temple, and breaking bread from house to house, they ate their food with gladness and simplicity of heart, praising God and having favor with all the people. And the Lord added to the church daily those who were being saved* (Acts 2:46-47).

My daughter, Rose, is an amazing young lady. She never lets anything "rain on her parade". She has been that way since she was a little girl. She is one of the most optimistic, joyful, loving people I know. She has a genuine faith in God and a healthy self-confidence that she can achieve anything she puts her hand to.

Rose is a person of great focus as well. I suppose I should not be surprised. When she was born, Deede and I were heavily involved as leaders in a local church in San Diego. She was practically raised on the front row of our little church! This doesn't seem to have had any ill effects. Rose is a true worshiper, always engaged in singing and praising the Lord. Even as a little girl, she took better notes from the pastor than most of the adults! Later, when my wife and I started traveling in ministry throughout the country, she traveled with us. So it is no surprise that she is a born leader and a real "go getter". Rose might say that she learned a lot from her parents, but there are a couple of things she did not learn from me. As a parent, I have been blessed through her gifts and witness.

I admire and respect Rose's musical and singing gifts. She definitely got neither of these from me. Probably her mother! Some sing like nightingales, and others... like gales in the night! I qualify for the latter. But, all joking aside, Rose is a gifted musician and songwriter, writing as many as five songs in a day! She also has had two worship bands. That is a gift from God.

Another thing I have gained from Rose's witness is the art of community. This lesson was learned after our family moved to a new home in Dallas, Texas. I took on a part-time pastoral role that soon became a full-time role. She joined the young adults ministry and was soon one of its key leaders.

Being a genuine "Pied Piper", it was not long before events and meetings were being scheduled for most weekends in our home. She was frequently on the phone with young people seeking her spiritual counsel. I remember one occasion when she left the house at one in the morning and drove across town to pick up a young person whose car had broken down and was stranded alongside the road. I was naturally concerned that it was too late for her to be receiving this type of call. But she did not seem to mind. She was committed to being a servant-leader for her group.

I also remember all the young people who frequently gathered in our home to have a place to "connect" with "family". I found out later that a stable home environment was not common with many of them. Our home became a home away from home.

These gatherings at our house were more than just "a place to hang out", they had meaning and purpose, and provided a place for a good hot meal. Often ten or fifteen gathered in our living room for Bible studies, work on new worship songs, or planning the next overseas mission trip. They even celebrated birthdays, engagements, or just-married couples with a special day together. In the truest sense of the word, they were a community.

## True Community

A true community is a group who are committed to growing and learning to do life together. They are committed to holding each other accountable spiritually for their daily walk and witness for Jesus Christ. As a matter of fact, one of the significant words in the New Testament that describes true followers of Jesus' lifestyle is "one another". At least eleven different exhortations are given to live out the "one another" principle.

> *The believers met in the Temple everyday. They ate together in their homes, happy to share their food with joyful hearts. They praised God and were liked by all the people. Everyday the Lord added those who were being saved to the group of believers* (Acts 2:46-47 NCV).

The soul of the Church is about people, people who have embraced each other by faith in a Person, the Lord Jesus Christ, and are endeavoring to live by His words and example. They recognize that God has done a miracle by His Spirit in their hearts and lives, being "baptized by one Spirit into the Body of Christ" (Ephesians 4; I Corinthians 12, 14).

Having experienced the miracle of His life, they also experience the miracle of His love toward one another. This creates a spiritual magnetic force field in which those outside of the family of God are drawn in by a desire to know Jesus in a similar way. This is what happened with the first believers. Their experiences were not a Sunday morning phenomenon but a daily encounter with Christ and a daily "adding" of those being saved to the Church.

**Jesus Builds His Church**

How does Jesus build His Church? What are some clear signs that the Holy Spirit is doing a supernatural work versus human beings doing a superficial work? Let me state it in a negative way first. The Church is not a club, where people pay their dues and elect officers and show up from time to time to keep up their club membership. The Church is not a building. Today, in our culture, the word "church" is almost synonymous with the place of meeting versus the people who meet in the place. We have forgotten that for the first three hundred years of Church history, people had no permanent headquarters in which to hold their services. No one could walk down the street with his friend and point to a building and say, "That's my church." This is the reason the scriptures record that they met publicly and in homes.

Stated positively, the true work of the Holy Spirit is the gift of faith. When Peter preached the first sermon on the Day of Pentecost, over 3,000 publicly put their trust in Jesus Christ (Acts 2:14-41). Faith is demonstrated by an act of obedience, which was evidenced on that day by their repentance and being baptized in water. They were giving witness to Jesus Christ and the fact that they now belonged to the family of God (Ephesians 2:8-10; Romans 8:16; Galatians 4:6-7).

The Church is a community of the faithful. Those who believed started to spend time with the people of God for spiritual growth and direction. "They continued steadfastly in the apostles' doctrine and fellowship, in breaking of bread and prayers" (Acts 2:42). They submitted themselves to the apostolic and local leadership in order that they might understand from the scriptures how to live this new life, and how to encourage others who were endeavoring to be true to the Lord Jesus.

In addition, they celebrated a covenant meal together. It was called a "love feast," where believers shared a common meal and then celebrated the "Lord's Supper," also known as the Eucharist or Communion. Then they prayed together for the needs among them and for those who were not present with them to be strengthened and "stay true to the Lord" in the face of problems and persecution. The writer to the Hebrew Christians wrote the following:

> "Let us hold fast the confession of our hope without wavering, for He who promised, is faithful. And let us consider one another in order to stir up love and good works, not forsaking the assembling of ourselves together, as is the manner of some, but exhorting one another, and so much the more as you see the Day approaching" (Hebrews 10:23-25).

Their new faith walk was demonstrated by caring and sharing with one another, along with mutual compassion and concern.

*Now all who believed were together, and had all things in common, and sold their possessions and goods and divided them among all, as anyone had need* (Acts 2:44-45).

This was the new community for which our Lord Jesus prayed before He went back to the Father (John 17). This new community, led by the Holy Spirit's direction, began to rapidly influence their culture. The status quo was dramatically affected, and many turned to the Lord Jesus.

The Church as a "new creation" order in the earth set the pace, affecting its culture on every level, spiritually as well as socially (see 2 Corinthians 5:17). Jesus told His first disciples as much in the Gospel of Matthew.

*You are the salt of the earth; but if the salt loses its flavor, how shall it be seasoned? It is then good for nothing but to be thrown out and trampled underfoot by men. You are the light of the world. A city that is set on a hill cannot be hidden. Nor do they light a lamp and put it under a basket, but on a lampstand, and it gives light to all who are in the house. Let your light so shine before men, that they may see your good works and glorify your Father in heaven* (Matthew 5:13-16).

The Church is called to redeem culture in the name of Jesus Christ for the glory of God the Father. The Church is to demonstrate that Jesus is, as Reinhold Niebuhr stated, "the Christ of Culture." He is to be seen as Christ in culture—"You are the salt of the earth." He is to be seen as Christ above culture—"You are the light of the world." He is to be seen as Christ transforming culture—"You are a city set on a hill which cannot be hid."

This is the Church for which Jesus died. She is to be so winsome and full of life that the words of the prophet Isaiah are fulfilled.

> *Many people shall come and say, "Come, and let us go up to the mountain of the LORD. To the house of the God of Jacob; He will teach us His ways, and we shall walk in His paths." For out of Zion shall go forth the law, and the word of the LORD from Jerusalem. He shall judge between the nations, and rebuke many people; they shall beat their swords into plowshares, and their spears into pruning hooks; nation shall not lift up sword against nation, neither shall they learn war anymore* (Isaiah 2:3-4).

**Let the Church** *be the Church* in this hour.

# *The* SOUL *of the Kingdom*

## Chapter Eleven

*Then the seventh angel sounded: And there were loud voices in heaven, saying, 'The kingdoms of this world have become the kingdoms of our Lord and of His Christ, and He shall reign forever and ever!' And the twenty-four elders who sat before God on their thrones fell on their faces and worshiped God, saying: 'We give You thanks, O Lord God Almighty, the One who is and who was and who is to come, because You have taken Your great power and reigned* (Revelation 11:15-17).

Leonard Ravenhill was my friend and mentor for almost seven years. He was as rare an individual as I have ever known, and was an even *rarer* man of God. When I first met him, he was already in his seventies, short and spry. But the two things that stand out the most in my mind are his gentle yet piercing eyes, and slender, bony fingers; I thought if he pointed one of them toward me, flames from heaven might shoot out! In private, he was the meekest man I have ever been around, but in the pulpit, his preaching was like a lion, bold and fearless!

Leonard's reputation as one of the illustrious revivalists of his time had been well established. He had ministered for over fifty years, and seen many great things done by God. He never tried to impress you with his spiritual exploits. As a matter of fact, I never remember him talking about himself at all. He always talked to me about God—often for hours at a time. But a pastor friend told me of an "eye witness" account of one of those mighty moves of God in England where, due to Leonard's ministry, the town buses had to be rerouted! Enormous crowds had gathered outdoors to hear the Word of God. Hundreds were won to the Lord.

On another occasion, Martha, Leonard's wife, told of seeing five people who were crippled and in wheelchairs stand up—healed! This was in the course of a communion service Leonard was conducting. No one had prayed for them. The power and presence of God simply touched them during the service! Again, in talking with one of his sons, I found it was quite common to hear of miracles of healing that were present while he was praying.

Leonard has been in the Lord's presence for a number of years. I still miss the fellowship I enjoyed with him, and the many prayers he offered for me. I am, to this very hour, challenged by his life and memory. I have often reflected upon his life, and have asked myself, "What was the secret of such an extraordinary life?" Two things that stand out in my mind were so characteristic of him: his passion for God and his life of prayer.

He would often express to me the passion of his heart, "Nobody thinks you can have too much money, too many cars or other things. But if someone gets serious about God and the things of His kingdom, loses sleep to pray, saves his money to sow it into missions work, or gives up a comfortable career to follow the call of God, then people declare, 'You're too extreme!'"

He cared very little about and did not fear the opinion of men. What mattered to him was God's opinion. For him, there was no compromise when it came to the kingdom of God. God is worthy of our very best at all times.

To say that he was "a man of prayer" was not an overstatement. Leonard breathed prayer as naturally as breathing air. I had the privilege of praying with him whenever we were together. I learned after his death, from a family member, that he routinely prayed ten hours a day. Although I did not know of his ten-hours-a-day prayer habit, I did know when he was praying for me, no matter where I might be in the country! For himself, he prayed only that he could be used more by God. His chief subject in prayer was the advancement of the kingdom of God in the earth.

**The Kingdom of God's Triumph**
While attending a prayer gathering for ministers in which Leonard was the facilitator, I recall his making this comment: "I've lived long enough to have seen no less than twenty earthly kingdoms pass away. They are no more." Then, with a wry smile, and full of joy he proclaimed, "But, although kingdoms may come to an end, the kingdom of God will last forever!"

Leonard was merely echoing what the prophet Daniel received in vision and understanding thousands of years prior, "…the God of heaven will set up a kingdom which shall never be destroyed; and the kingdom shall not be left to other people… it shall stand forever" (Daniel 2:44). John, the beloved apostle, is given a vision expressing the same,

"The kingdoms of this world have become the kingdoms of our Lord and of His Christ, and He shall reign forever and ever!" (Revelation 11:15).

The announcement of God's unending kingdom is a fact that is not predicated or contingent upon a succession of royalty. The rightful heir is seated upon the throne now and forever in eternity.

There can be no abiding kingdom without an abiding king. The actual word "kingdom" presupposes a king is in residence. It means "the realm or dominion of the king". If you follow the narrative story found in the Bible, you soon discover there was a kingdom mindset given from the beginning. At the dawn of the creation story, God created men and women to rule upon the earth. Although temporarily forfeited due to their fall, the purpose of God declared in the Garden continued to be anticipated through Moses and the Prophets (Genesis 1:26-28; Genesis 49:10 ; Isaiah 9:6-7; Zechariah 9:9-10).

**The Cry for a King**

The nation of Israel, mistaking that its actual need for protection and defending would come from an earthly king like those of the other nations around them, cried out to the prophet Samuel, "Give us a king like the other nations!"(1 Samuel 8). In their search for an earthly king, they were rejecting God's sovereign right to rule. However, God was not deterred. The day would come when He would place His king on the throne. That day dawned at the birth of Jesus Christ, God's Son, given through the womb of the Virgin Mary.

His right to rule the earth was immediately challenged by King Herod. Herod was Rome's choice as appointed king over the Jews. When he got wind of "He who is born king of the Jews" from the three kings, the Wise Men from the East, he ordered that the child should be found and exterminated. His murderous plans did not succeed, for God protected the child, albeit the holocaust of innocent Jewish children was the fruit of his efforts. For the next thirty odd years, Jesus was hidden away wrapped in a shroud of silence. Then one day, the silence was broken, as he preached to the people of Galilee, "Repent: for the kingdom of heaven is at hand!" (Matthew 4:17).

**The Nature of the Kingdom**
Every kingdom represents the character of the king, as the king's nature will permeate his kingdom for either good or evil. God's kingdom is righteous. Righteousness is a manifestation of things made right or done right, and speaks of moral and upright living. His kingdom is also known by peace, the inner sense of quietness and rest when war has ceased. Those who are a part of His kingdom know His peace personally and seek to advance His peace as peacemakers in the earth.

His kingdom is a kingdom of joy. Joy is not dependent on happy circumstances, but is a gift from God, a deep sense of inner cheerfulness. Even when things around us seem to be out of control, we know that God is still in control. Again, God's kingdom is truth, that reality revealed by God through His Son who declared, "I am the way, the truth and the life" (John 14:6). Truth is His holy standard found in His Word. The prophet Isaiah reminds us, "The grass withers, the flower fades, but the Word of God abides forever" (Isaiah 40:8).

God's kingdom is also a kingdom of justice. "Righteousness and justice are the foundation of Your throne" (Psalm 89:14). Righteousness is the expression of the character of the kingdom of God; justice is the process and means by which it is established. There is a cry for justice and peace in the earth as never before. Though all may not yet acknowledge it, this cry among the nations is for the one true and righteous King.

## A Kingdom of Power

No kingdom can stand without the power to establish its claim to allegiance and obedience. God's kingdom reigns not only out of the good will of the people but also because "the kingdom is not in word but in power"(1 Corinthians 4:20). The early followers of Christ witnessed this fact. They understood that after Jesus rose from the dead and ascended into heaven, He would sit on the right hand of the power of God, the Father. Therefore, even though God's people were opposed in the earth, they refused to be intimidated, and they never lost heart (Acts 4). They joined together in prayer and claimed God's promises of Jesus' present reign over all rulers of the earth as recorded in the psalms of David.

> *Why do the nations rage, and the people plot a vain thing? The kings of the earth set themselves, and the rulers take counsel together, against the LORD and against His Anointed, saying, "Let us break their bonds in pieces and cast away their cords from us."*
>
> *He who sits in the heavens shall laugh; the LORD shall hold them in derision. Then He shall speak to them in His wrath, and distress them in His deep displeasure: "Yet I have set My King on My holy hill of Zion."*

> *"I will declare the decree: The LORD has said to Me, 'You are My son, today I have begotten You. Ask of Me, and I will give You the nations for Your inheritance, and the ends of the earth for Your possession. You shall break them with a rod of iron; you shall dash them to pieces like a potter's vessel.'"*
>
> *Now therefore, be wise, O kings; be instructed, you judges of the earth. Serve the LORD with fear, and rejoice with trembling. Kiss the Son, lest He be angry, and you perish in the way, when His wrath is kindled but a little* (Psalm 2).

This prayer is being answered today! God is pouring out His power once again, extending the message of His kingdom even to the uttermost parts of the earth.

The reign of Jesus Christ is the only hope for the world. He is the soul of the Kingdom. The prophet Isaiah magnificently records the hope and promise of His reign.

> *For unto us a Child is born, unto us a Son is given; and the government will be upon His shoulder. And His name will be called Wonderful, Counselor, Mighty God, Everlasting Father, Prince of Peace. Of the increase of His government and peace there will be no end, upon the throne of David and over His kingdom, to order it and establish it with judgment and justice from that time forward, even forever. the zeal of the Lord of hosts will perform this* (Isaiah 9:6-7).

The reign of Jesus is what Leonard Ravenhill was so passionate about. His prayers for the Kingdom of God were never ceasing. This is what we are called to seek with all our heart, a kingdom of righteousness. May we add our prayers to those of his and all those who surround the throne, and with all those who long for His appearing. *Maranatha!*